Blackwater

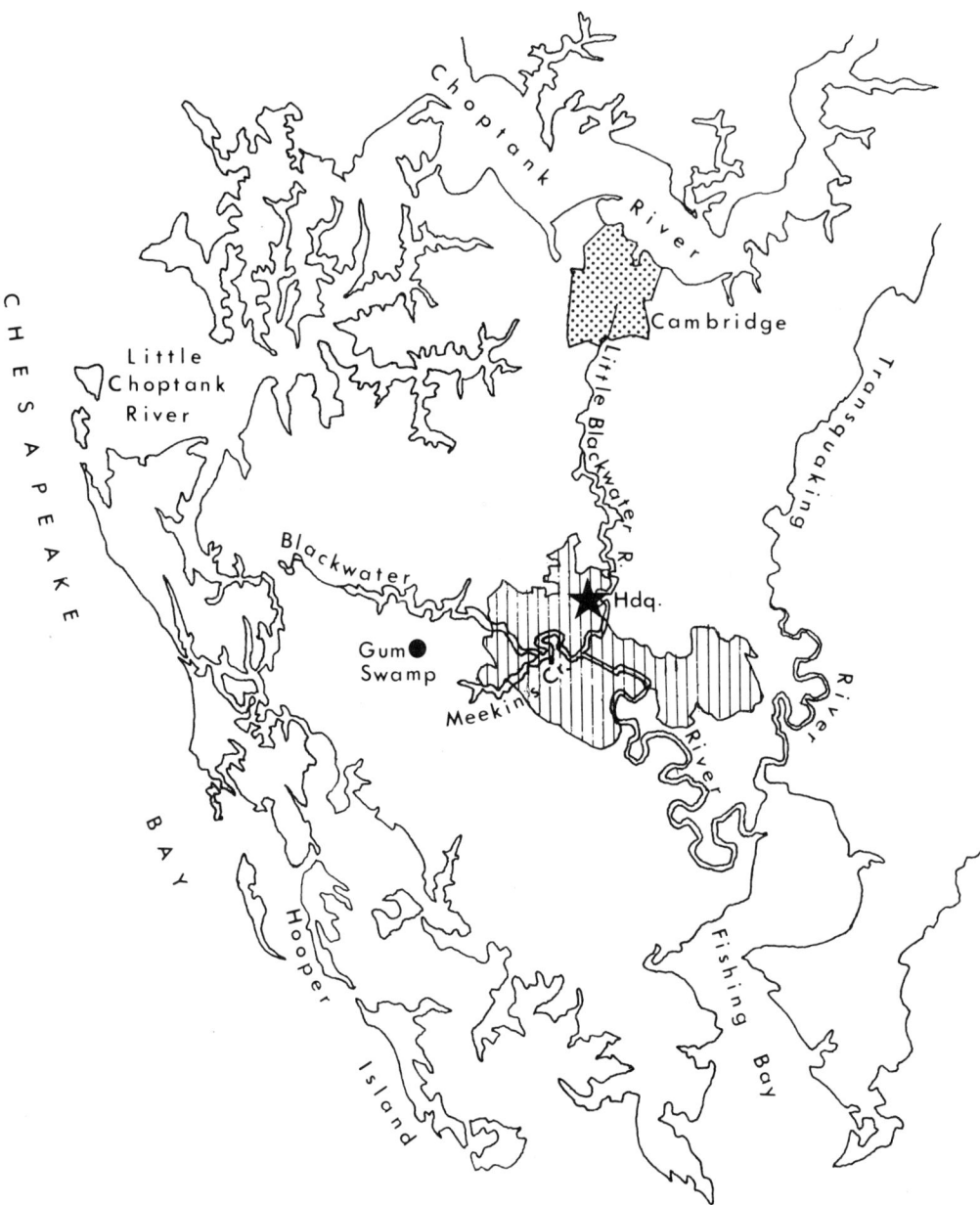

Blackwater—large shaded area is Blackwater National Wildlife Refuge.

Brooke Meanley

Blackwater

TIDEWATER PUBLISHERS
Cambridge   Maryland
1978

Copyright © 1978, by Tidewater Publishers

All Rights Reserved

No part of this book may be used or reproduced in any manner whatsoever without written permission except in the case of brief quotations embodied in critical articles and reviews. For information address Tidewater Publishers, Cambridge, Md. 21613

Library of Congress Cataloging in Publication Data

Meanley, Brooke.
   Blackwater.

   Bibliography: p.
   Includes index.
   1. Zoology--Maryland--Blackwater. 2. Birds--Maryland--Blackwater. 3. Blackwater National Wildlife Refuge, Md. I. Title.
QL182.M4   599'.09752'27   78-35
ISBN 0-87033-245-7

Printed and Bound in the United States of America

Contents

Frontispiece ii
Acknowledgments vii
Introduction ix

Blackwater and Its Marshes 1
Canada Geese from Ungava 10
The Snow Goose 16
Bald Eagles, Their Nests and Foods at Blackwater 19
Tidemarsh Muskrats 26
The Nutria 32
The Delmarva Fox Squirrel 34
Breeding Birds of the Loblolly Pine Woods 39
On the Trail of the Red-Cockaded Woodpecker 48
The Timberdoodle 53
The Atlantic Blue-Winged Teal 57
Breeding Birds of Blackwater Marshes 59
Foods of Marsh Ducks 79
Birds of Prey of the Marshes 85
Otters, Deer, and Raccoons of the Brackish Marshes . . . 89
The Swamp Owl 92
Spring and Fall Migration of Birds at Blackwater 98
The Christmas Bird Count in Southern Dorchester County . 104
The Whistling Swan on the Wintering Ground 113
Winter of '77 118
Rare Occurrences of Birds at Blackwater 124

Appendix I
   Southern Dorchester County Christmas Bird Count . . . 133

Appendix II
  Common and Scientific Names of:
    Birds 137
    Mammals 139
    Other Animals 139
    Plants 139
Bibliography 140
Index 143

Acknowledgments

I wish to thank the following friends, some of them colleagues of mine in the U.S. Fish and Wildlife Service, who have supplied information, photographs, and other favors for the production of this manuscript: William H. Julian, Guy Willey, Peter J. Van Huizen, Bob Hines, Chandler S. Robbins, Robert E. Stewart, Tony Florio, Matt Perry, Sam Grimes, Marshall Howe, Luther Goldman, Gorman Bond, Mike Haramis, Danny Bystrak, Elizabeth Bell, John W. Taylor, and Francis Uhler.

Thanks also are due Robert Arbib, editor of *American Birds*, a publication of the National Audubon Society, for permission to publish Christmas Bird Count data for southern Dorchester County; and to Elizabeth Caulk, editor of the *Delaware Conservationist*, for permission to use a poem that appeared in that magazine.

I am indebted to my wife, Anna Gilkeson Meanley, who has kindly reviewed the manuscript.

Black and white sketches are by Bob Hines, courtesy of the U.S. Fish and Wildlife Service, and by John W. Taylor, Chesapeake Bay waterfowl artist. Photographs are by the author unless otherwise credited.

BROOKE MEANLEY

Introduction

The extensive marshlands and bordering loblolly pine forests of southern Dorchester County, Maryland, form one of the best areas for wildlife in the Chesapeake Bay Country. Enhancing this already rich wildlife area is the 11,000-acre Blackwater National Wildlife Refuge established in its midst in 1933 (Figs. 1 and 2).

Fig. 1. Vegetation surrounding the Blackwater Refuge sign is Phragmites. It is mainly a marsh edge plant in the Blackwater area, but in some sections of the Chesapeake Bay Country it forms extensive pure stands, and is mainly considered a pest plant, although it affords cover for some wildlife.

Among Blackwater's distinguishing features as a wildlife area are, 1) the highest population density of nesting bald eagles in the eastern United States north of Florida, 2) the largest population of Delmarva fox squirrels extant, 3) a major concentration area of Canada geese along the Atlantic Flyway, 4) one of the most important muskrat producing areas in the United States, and 5) the northern limit of the range of the red-cockaded woodpecker (and only known nesting area in Maryland).

From the beginning I have followed the development of Blackwater Refuge with great interest; and all the more because a number of my friends and colleagues in the U.S. Fish and Wildlife Service have played an important role in its development.

Fig. 2. Blackwater country. The Refuge is comprised of 11,627 acres, including 5,700 acres of marsh, 4,100 acres of open water, 1,224 acres of maritime loblolly pine forest, and 603 acres of potential cropland. Photograph courtesy of Blackwater National Wildlife Refuge.

Francis Uhler (Fig. 3) made the original wildlife and marsh assessments, and Peter J. Van Huizen (Fig. 4) made the first land surveys and was the first manager. William H. Julian, the present manager, is a longtime friend from the days when we worked on different wildlife projects in Louisiana. Cornelius Wallace, manager at Blackwater for 20 years, and Guy Willey, biologist for 25 years, played significant roles, along with others, in the development of the Refuge as a major link in the chain of national waterfowl refuges along the Atlantic Flyway.

Ornithologists who have made important contributions to our knowledge of the birds of the Blackwater area are: Ralph Jackson of Cambridge, Maryland, the pioneer naturalist in the region who published an article entitled "Breeding Birds of the Cambridge Area, Maryland" (1) (including the Blackwater area), based mainly on his

Note: Numbers in parentheses are references to the Bibliography, page 140.

Introduction

Fig. 3. Francis M. Uhler, U.S. Fish and Wildlife Service biologist, collecting submerged aquatic plant foods of waterfowl from brackish marsh pond. Photograph courtesy of U.S. Fish and Wildlife Service.

and Harry N. Harrison's investigations in the first quarter of this century; Talbot Denmead, a Baltimore ornithologist of the same period, who took notes on birds when he hunted and fished in the area, and published reports in the *Maryland Conservationist*, of which he was editor at one time; Frank Smith, one of the first biologists at the Refuge, who conducted important studies of bald eagles and red-cockaded woodpeckers; Chandler S. Robbins who has coordinated most of the Christmas bird counts in southern Dorchester County during the last 30 years; and Robert E. Stewart who conducted avian ecology studies for many years.

Fig. 4. Peter J. Van Huizen was the first manager at Blackwater National Wildlife Refuge (1933-1937). Photograph was made at Blackwater in the spring of 1976.

Frank Smith, Herbert Dozier, and Van T. Harris, biologists with the U.S. Fish and Wildlife Service or its predecessor agency, the U.S. Biological Survey, made important studies of muskrats of Blackwater marshes.

In this report I am covering, in addition to the Refuge's 11,000 acres, the surrounding area drained by the Blackwater, Little Blackwater, and the Transquaking Rivers.

The following publications have been especially helpful in developing this manuscript: *Muskrat Investigations in Dorchester County, Maryland,* 1930-1934, by Frank Smith (2); *Waterfowl Populations in the Upper Chesapeake Region,* by Robert E. Stewart (3); and *Birds of Maryland and the District of Columbia,* by Robert E. Stewart and Chandler S. Robbins (4).

Blackwater and Its Marshes

Along the road leading south from the town of Cambridge, Maryland, in the direction of Hooper Island and Bishop's Head, farmland gradually disappears as we approach a broad belt of marshland laced with waterways and interrupted with islands of loblolly pine. In a general way, one might be reminded of the Everglades of southern Florida, an extensive sawgrass marsh with tree islands or hammocks.

This section of southern Dorchester County is known as "Blackwater," after the dark-colored river that winds through the marshes and empties into Fishing Bay. The Blackwater (Fig. 5) flows from three swamps lying at the head of the marshes. These swamps, Gum, Kentuck, and Moneystump, the bordering loblolly pine forests, and the peaty soil of the marshes, apparently are the reason for the dark-colored water of the river. Farther south on the Coastal Plain almost all waters flowing from swamps are dark. Blackwater National Wildlife Refuge lies in the heart of this country.

The vast marshlands of the Blackwater are the dominating features of the landscape (Fig. 6). Such marshes have developed on broad, shallow estuarine flats that are flooded by the tides, and are located near large bodies of water like Fishing Bay or the Chesapeake. The upper reaches of the Blackwater and Little Blackwater Rivers, Meekins Creek, and the Transquaking River are mostly fresh (Fig. 7); along the lower portion of these rivers the marshes are generally brackish, a result of intrusion of opposing forces of saltwater from the Bay and freshwater from the rivers.

Allen Bobwill (5), in the following description, elucidates the contradictory ebbs and flows which in their continual alternation maintain these "transitional" marshes.

"This slowly sinking land is continuously being overrun by the waters backed up by the tidal action of the salty Chesapeake Bay, tending to make this section a salt marsh. The Blackwater River, however, with its tributaries, is continuously pouring out its slow flood of silt-bearing fresh water, which flows softly and gently down through this wide water-covered section, slowly dropping its burden of fine mud and silt over the whole area. This silt is caught and held by the tangled roots and living vegetation of the marsh plants, which, with the river, serve as important agencies in building up the land.

"So, here, we have four forces—the sinking land, the salty baywater, the silt-bearing river, and soil-building plant life. These forces are waging a slow war against each other, two trying to make it an area of water, and two trying to build more land.

"However, there is still another struggle going on here, on the wide marshlands. This is the constant war for dominance between the salt water of the bay, and fresh water of the Blackwater river. Exceptionally high tides, and drought years, or periods of little rainfall, result in increased saltiness of the marshes, as additional water seeps in from the bay. Heavy spring rains, or other periods of excessive rainfall result in an extra amount of fresh water and silt coming down from the Blackwater.

"This fluctuation in saltiness bears directly upon the plant life of the marshes...."

Note: Numbers in parentheses are references to the Bibliography, page 140.

Fig. 5. Blackwater River winding through the marshland toward Fishing Bay, May 1976.

Fig. 6. A typical Blackwater scene: Olney three-square brackish marsh, loblolly pine forest, muskrat house in the marsh, and bald eagle nest in a pine tree. Blackwater Refuge, spring 1976.

Fig. 7. Fresh Bay marsh, upper section of Blackwater River. Vegetation mainly consists of narrowleaf cattail, Olney three-square, and switchgrass. White waterlilies in the pond are indicators of fresh water, June 1960.

Fig. 8. Transquaking River showing slightly brackish tidal marsh approximately five miles northeast of Blackwater Refuge. Predominant aquatic plants of the marsh are Olney three-square, softstem bulrush, and narrowleaf cattail. Characteristic breeding birds are the red-winged blackbird, long-billed marsh wren, king rail, Virginia rail, least bittern, and common gallinule, June 1976.

Fig. 9. Wild rice. In Maryland, the seed of this plant matures in early September, and at that time is a prime food of the blue-winged teal, sora, bobolink, and red-winged blackbird. A small patch was present along the upper reaches of the Transquaking River at DeCoursey Bridge, Dorchester County, in the summer of 1975. The following summer, due to a drought, the water was too salty at that station for wild rice.

This point is well illustrated by events at the DeCoursey Bridge marsh along the Transquaking River a few miles east of Blackwater Refuge (Fig. 8). In the summer of 1975, a small patch of wild rice, which grows in fresh and slightly brackish water, was noted near the bridge (Fig. 9). A year later there was no wild rice, but in its place, a few plants of saltmarsh cordgrass, a plant of higher salinities. This change was no doubt due to the shortage of rainfall in the spring of 1976. Wild rice can stand a moderate degree of brackishness, extending downstream where the water during high tide is a little more than one-fifth as saline as average sea water.

Olney three-square or three-cornered sedge is the predominant plant of Blackwater's marshlands. A prime muskrat and goose food, three-square grows mostly in

Fig. 10. A three-square marsh burning on a winter evening. Trappers burn the marsh to make walking easier.

Fig. 11. Saltmeadow cordgrass at Blackwater is important nesting habitat of the black duck, blue-winged teal, willet, black rail, and sharp-tailed and seaside sparrows.

poorly drained areas. When Van T. Harris, of the U.S. Fish and Wildlife Service, was engaged in muskrat research in the Olney three-square at Blackwater in 1949-51, he reported that water in the marshes ranged from 2 to 42 percent of average sea salinity. Thus most of the marshlands at Blackwater are brackish.

Because of the importance to several of Blackwater's key wildlife species, three-square is maintained, when necessary, by various forms of management, including burning (Fig. 10). Annual burning prevents other aquatic plant species from displacing three-square; provides green food for geese during late winter and early spring (thus producing a buffer against feeding in winter wheat fields); and concentrates the introduced nutria, a mammal larger than a muskrat that likes fairly dense cover and which must be kept under control. Trappers also burn to facilitate their own mobility in the marsh.

Important secondary plant species of the Blackwater River marsh are narrowleaf cattail, saltmeadow cordgrass (Fig. 11), and saltmarsh cordgrass. All three are key indicators of their environment. Cattail is restricted to areas where the water level is

Fig. 12. Rose mallow or hibiscus (large flower in foreground) and saltmarsh mallows in slightly brackish marsh along the Transquaking River near DeCoursey Bridge, August. Other vegetation is mostly narrowleaf cattail. This habitat is optimum for nesting king rails and several other species of marsh birds.

fairly stable and mostly fresh; saltmeadow cordgrass occupies brackish areas where the land is a little higher and is flooded only by exceptionally high tides; and saltmarsh cordgrass occurs along the lower reaches of the Blackwater River toward Fishing Bay. Each of these marsh communities has its key bird species, probably best exemplified by the rails. The king rail is associated mainly with fresh and slightly brackish marshes composed of fairly tall plants, the black rail with salt meadows, and the clapper rail with saltmarsh cordgrass.

The Transquaking River marsh in the DeCoursey Bridge area has the greatest variety of aquatic plants that I have observed in southern Dorchester County. The marsh is greenest in June, and probably most attractive in August when the rose mallow, or hibiscus, and the saltmarsh mallow are in bloom (Fig. 12). Olney three-

Fig. 13. Big cordgrass, brackish water plant, growing beside tidal gut that leads into the Transquaking River near Bestpitch. Plants reach seven or eight feet in height, providing some of the best cover for marsh birds, as the life-form of the plant persists throughout most of the year. It is important as nesting habitat for long-billed marsh wrens, as escape and loafing cover for king rails that feed along the edge of tidal guts at low tide, and as roosting cover for red-winged blackbirds. A roost of over a million red-winged blackbirds was located in the Bestpitch marsh in January 1964.

Fig. 14. Marsh denuded by Canada and snow geese at Blackwater Refuge. Bare foreground area of peat was formerly covered with Olney three-square marsh, as seen in background.

square, narrowleaf cattail, and softstem bulrush were the predominant plants at this station in the spring and summer of 1976. Other aquatic plants observed included common three-square, twigrush, Phragmites, spikerush, pickerelweed, big cordgrass, tidemarsh water hemp, and dotted smartweed. Approximately two miles downstream at Bestpitch, where the water is more brackish, big cordgrass is the predominant marsh plant (Fig. 13).

In the opinion of Francis Uhler, who made extensive studies of the Blackwater area in the early 1930s, the marshlands have changed little in the last 45 years. Some bare areas in the marsh may be the result of subsidence, and some sections of three-square marsh have been denuded either by periodic muskrat "eatouts," moth larvae, or by the increasing Canada goose population (Fig. 14).

An interesting recent development has been the winter occurrence of several thousand lesser snow geese (white and blue color phases). In the winter of 1975-76, an estimated 3,500 of these traditional Mississippi and Central Flyway migrants visited Blackwater. Lesser snows are more damaging to the marsh than Canadas as their diggings are more devastating. However, a certain amount of denuding of the marsh by geese and muskrats effects more interspersion, and the more diversified habitat attracts a greater variety of birdlife.

Blackwater and Its Marshes

Fig. 15. View to the south from dike along wildlife drive at Blackwater National Wildlife Refuge. The ponds and marshes shown are feeding and rest areas for virtually every species of waterfowl that visits Blackwater (28 have been reported). Dead pines in the marsh are favorite perches of wintering bald eagles, September 1976.

When flushed by tides, "eatouts," or openings in the marsh, become ponds where herons, egrets, ibises, shorebirds (especially yellowlegs, dunlins, and snipe), and waterfowl forage for amphibians, crustaceans, mollusks, minnows, and mosquito larvae.

Blackwater country will probably change very little in the next 45 years. It may get a little wetter. The few dead loblolly pines stranded a short distance from shore out in the marsh probably got their start from seeds deposited on dry land (Fig. 15).

Canada Geese from Ungava

In recent years more Canada geese have been wintering on the Eastern Shore of Maryland than in any other locality in North America. According to Bellrose (6), during the period 1970-1975, the Mid-Atlantic population of Canada geese wintered as follows: central and western New York, 8,000; western Pennsylvania, 26,000; Delaware and Maryland (Delmarva Peninsula), 537,000; coastal Virginia, 60,000; North Carolina 58,000; and South Carolina 10,500.

A large segment of the goose population wintering in the Chesapeake Bay Country formerly wintered farther south, particularly along the Outer Coastal Plain of North Carolina. The so-called "short-stopping" of many geese somewhat farther north of the former range is due mostly to the introduction of the mechanical corn picker, which leaves as much as ten percent of the crop in the field. Also, farmers on the Eastern Shore are now growing more corn, and they plow in the spring, whereas in eastern North Carolina farmers grow as much corn as ever, but have changed from spring to fall plowing, and are thus turning under some of the residual crop. An example of the increase in Canada geese is seen in population figures at Blackwater

Fig. 16. Canada geese of the Atlantic Flyway weigh from six to nine pounds (rarely ten), depending upon sex and age. Important foods of Canadas in the Blackwater area are native grasses, sedges and waste corn. Photograph by Rex Gary Schmidt, U.S. Fish and Wildlife Service.

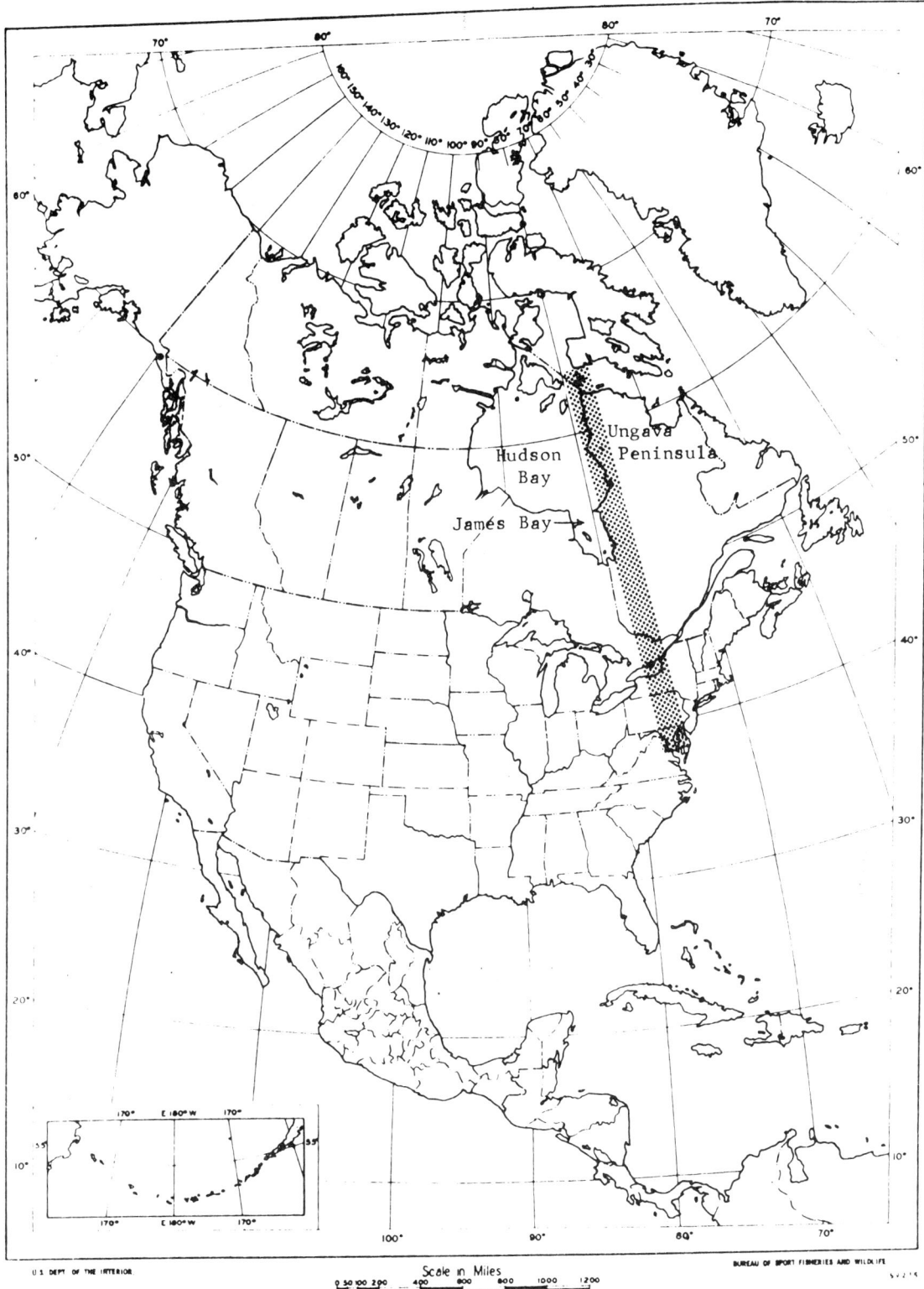

Fig. 17. Main migration corridor between nesting and wintering grounds of the Mid-Atlantic population of Canada geese.

National Wildlife Refuge. In the 1940s, approximately 5,000 geese visited the Refuge in winter; now the annual population is about 100,000 at the peak of migration.

Blackwater, the nearby lower Choptank River, Wye River area, and lower Chester River are the major concentration areas on the Eastern Shore.

Ornithologists have divided Canada geese into 12 fairly discreet populations (6). Each population generally has its own nesting and wintering grounds, and migration route that it follows to and from these areas. Geese in the central and eastern part of the continent are larger than those of the far western regions. The giant Canada goose of the mid-continent weighs up to 18 pounds, while the cackling Canada goose of the Pacific Coast weighs only three pounds. Chesapeake Bay geese weigh up to nine pounds (Fig. 16).

The geese that spend the winter at Blackwater belong to the Mid-Atlantic population that originates in the Ungava Peninsula, the land mass that lies between James and Hudson Bays, and the Atlantic Ocean (7) (Fig. 17).

While it would appear from recoveries of banded birds that most of the geese wintering at Blackwater nest along the eastern margin of James Bay and Hudson Bay, the fact that some banded birds have been recovered farther in the interior of Ungava would indicate that the breeding population is fairly widely distributed. The cluster of band recoveries near James and Hudson Bays is at least partly due to the Indian and Eskimo villages being located there (8). Cree Indians and Eskimos who depend on geese as part of their food source, are responsible for many of the recoveries of birds banded at Blackwater and elsewhere in the Chesapeake Bay Country. Also, the eastern boundary of James and Hudson Bays appears to be the main migration corridor of Canada geese that nest in Ungava.

Following the breeding season and summer molt, geese begin to stage in areas near the coast of James and Hudson Bays preparatory to migration southward. The main migration corridor south is through southern Quebec, across Lake Ontario into central New York, and down through eastern Pennsylvania to Chesapeake Bay.

The first birds arrive at Blackwater in late September, with numbers increasing through October until a peak population of 80,000-100,000 birds is reached in November. Some of the geese continue on to southeastern Virginia, eastern North Carolina, and South Carolina. A few scatter to other sections of the Chesapeake Bay, with some 30,000-40,000 remaining at Blackwater all winter (Figs. 18 and 19).

Geese are essentially grazing birds, which is one of the reasons why so many of them nest in the arctic tundra where the almost constant daylight and the moist substrate during the breeding season produce a luxuriant growth of tender grasses and sedges. On the wintering ground, as mentioned heretofore, they have shifted their foraging activity to some extent from the native marshlands to agricultural crop fields. While they will still feed on the stems and roots of three-square, the predominant plant of Blackwater marshes, they also glean the stubble fields for residue corn and soybeans left from the fall harvest, and browse the winter wheat fields and pasturelands. The whistling swans that are now doing the same may have

Fig. 18. Canada geese at the headquarters area, Blackwater National Wildlife Refuge. These wild geese that come from the far north tundra and muskeg country of the Canadian wilderness walk around the headquarters buildings at Blackwater like domestic fowl. They know when they are in a sanctuary. Photograph by Luther C. Goldman, U.S. Fish and Wildlife Service.

Fig. 19. Canada geese and a few lesser snow geese at Blackwater Refuge. The Canada goose population in the Chesapeake Bay area has increased by more than tenfold in recent years. The upswing in population began with the establishment and early management practices of the Blackwater National Wildlife Refuge. Photograph by Luther C. Goldman, U.S. Fish and Wildlife Service.

Fig. 20. Not a tree house, but a goose blind near Blackwater National Wildlife Refuge. Canada geese moving out of the Refuge to feed in nearby grain stubble fields fly low over the woods, sometimes within range of the hunter's tree-house blind.

picked up the habit from the geese because submerged aquatic plants, once a favorite food of swans, are presently in short supply.

During the hunting season, which is usually sometime between November 1 and January 15, some geese leave the Blackwater Refuge between 7:00 a.m. and 9:00 a.m. to feed in surrounding stubble fields as far as 10 to 15 miles away. Geese that move out during the day run the gauntlet of gunners that ring the Refuge, shooting from pits or standard-type duck blinds in stubble fields, and platforms in trees (Fig. 20).

As the gunning pressure increases they return to the Refuge to feed and loaf. Geese also feed away from the Refuge on moonlight nights. During stormy weather they tend to stay at the Refuge throughout the day.

Some of the geese begin leaving Blackwater for the north country before winter is over. Some flights are underway by the second week in February; and all are airborne northward during March. In migration they cruise at about 40 miles per hour, and cover about 50 miles a day unless it is late in the season and a longer flight has to be made to reach the nesting grounds on time. They usually travel at a height of 2,000-4,000 feet, but in mountainous country they are known to go above 10,000 feet. The vanguard arrives in the Hudson Bay area by about May 1.

Because geese nest in the far north country where weather conditions are fairly stable during the breeding season, where there is little interference from man, and where there are fewer predatory animals, they continue to prosper better than most species of ducks, so many of which are produced in the prairie pothole country of the Dakotas, Saskatchewan, and Manitoba where frequent droughts and the reclamation of wetlands for agriculture are having a depressing effect on the "duck factory."

The Snow Goose

Both greater and lesser snow geese occur in Maryland sometime during the winter-half of the year. The greater snow *(Anser caerulescens atlanticus)* occurs along the Atlantic Coast and the lesser snow *(Anser caerulescens caerulescens)*, winters mainly at Blackwater Refuge and vicinity. It may seem somewhat complex that both snow geese are varieties of the same species, termed subspecies or geographic races by the ornithologists; and that there are two color phases of the lesser snow goose, the white and the blue (Fig. 21); and further, that the blue-phase bird was considered to be a separate species known as the blue goose until recently when it was established that the two differently-colored birds interbreed on their arctic tundra nesting grounds. The English name, snow goose, has been retained, but the blue-phase bird is still usually referred to as the blue goose. Color phases occur in several North American species of birds, and in Maryland a good example is the screech owl, with

Fig. 21. Part of a flock of 1,200 snow geese and 80,000 Canada geese at Blackwater National Wildlife Refuge, November 3, 1976. The snow geese come mainly from Baffin Island or Southampton Island in the arctic tundra, and the Canada geese from east of Hudson and James Bays. Note white and blue color phases of the snow goose. Birds with white heads and necks and darkish bodies are the blue phase of the snow goose, often referred to as the blue goose.

rufous and gray phases. With the goose as with the owl, birds of two color phases or the same color may be mated. It is important to note that the greater snow goose and the lesser snow goose are discreet populations from different areas, and do not interbreed.

While the entire population (50,000-100,000) of the greater snow goose winters along the Middle Atlantic Coast, mainly from Chincoteague, Virginia, to northeastern North Carolina, the traditional wintering ground of the lesser snow goose is in the Lower Mississippi Valley, along the Texas coast, and in the Central Valley of California.

Until recent years lesser snow geese have been rather rare in the Atlantic Flyway, and while some 2,000-4,000 visit the Blackwater Refuge in the fall and winter, this number is only a fraction of the national population averaging 1,277,000 during 1955-1974 (6).

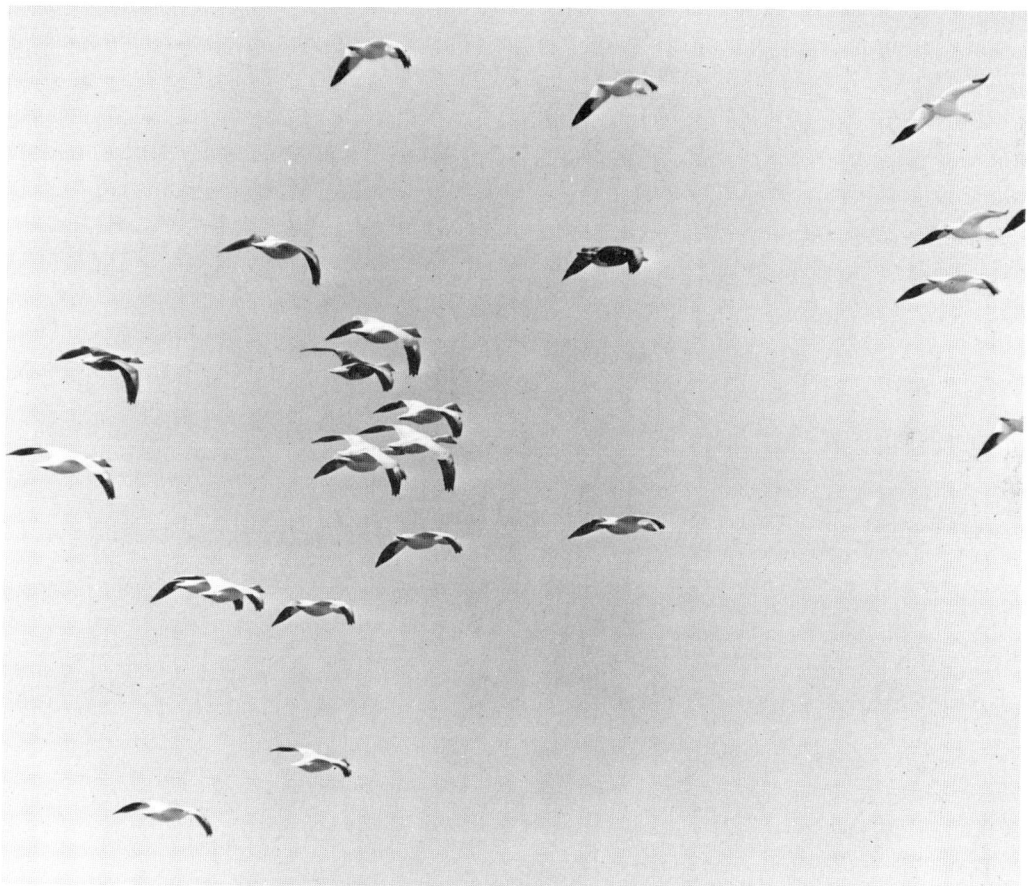

Fig. 22. Lesser snow geese that migrate from their eastern arctic nesting grounds to Chesapeake Bay, stage or assemble at the south end of Hudson Bay and James Bay in the latter half of September. On the flight south the birds fly higher than in the spring, sometimes up to 10,000 feet, but more often at 3,000—5,000. They usually arrive at Blackwater Refuge in the second half of October. Photograph by Luther C. Goldman, U.S. Fish and Wildlife Service.

Birds that winter at Blackwater apparently come from breeding grounds on Baffin Island in the eastern arctic area. Following summer molt they assemble at staging areas at the south end of Hudson Bay and James Bay in September (6). Migration southward begins in early October (Fig. 22), and by the latter part of the month they have arrived at Blackwater.

At Blackwater Refuge they feed mainly on fescue and other grasses planted for them, corn from stubble fields, and rootstocks of three-square from the native marsh. They are grubbers and grazers. In three-square marshes they dig and enlarge holes to get at the rhizomes. When they occasionally leave the Refuge they may pull up a few winter wheat sprouts. I have seen snow geese, whistling swans, and Canada geese feeding together in the same soybean stubble near Blackwater. In the Gulf Coast area of southwest Louisiana and contiguous Texas prairies where a major segment of the population occurs in winter, one of their main foods is waste grain left from the harvest operations in rice fields.

In the economy of man, migratory lesser snow geese that stage on the Hudson-James Bay coasts are important to the Indians. They use the feathers for making bedrolls, the fat in making bannock, and the remainder of the flesh and even the cleaned intestines for food, eaten fresh, dried, or smoked. In former times, spoons were made from the breastbones. The kill by the Indians has been about 35,000-75,000 annually (9).

Bald Eagles, Their Nests and Foods at Blackwater

Blackwater has the highest nesting density of bald eagles in the Chesapeake Bay Country. In the spring of 1976, there were four active nests on the Blackwater National Wildlife Refuge, and five in the area surrounding the Refuge.

The number of active nests on the Refuge varies slightly from year to year. In some years there may be as many as six nests. In 1974 and 1975, a nest along Egypt Road was barely outside of the Refuge boundary. After only two years of use, in 1976, the pair built a new nest on Refuge property approximately one-fourth of a mile from the old one.

Although there were many more nesting eagles in the Chesapeake Bay Country 40 or 50 years ago, it is doubtful that the number nesting in the Blackwater area was much greater than it is today. The Blackwater section of southern Dorchester County can support only so many breeding pairs of eagles. A pair requires a territory of at least a square mile.

Though there are some big hardwood trees in southern Dorchester County—oaks, gums, and others—loblolly pines are invariably selected for nest sites (Figs. 23 and 24). Guy Willey, who has worked at the Refuge for 25 years, and P.J. Van Huizen, who was there in the 1930s, tell me that every nest they have observed has been in a pine. The pines are probably chosen not only because they are the predominant trees and the best life-form for a nest site, but also because pines usually grow closer to the marshes and open water, principal hunting grounds of the eagle.

In the upper Chesapeake Bay region, most nests are in hardwoods near estuaries as there are no large loblolly pines in that area, and the indigenous Virginia pines seldom grow large enough to support an eagle's nest. I did see one in *Pinus virginiana* at Arnold, in Anne Arundel County, in the mid-1930s (Fig. 25).

Ornithological literature presents many examples of the size of eagle nests. Some in use for many years have been reported to weigh two tons.

Frank Smith weighed a nest at Gum Swamp in the Blackwater country in 1933. Smith describes the location of the nest and how its weight was determined in an interesting article in the *Auk* (10), a scientific ornithological journal:

"The nest was located some two hundred yards from the open marsh and less than a mile from Blackwater River. It was about seven miles to the waters of Chesapeake Bay and less than three quarters of a mile to the nearest house. The original nest had been located for no one knows how long in a big pine far back in the swamp. Some thirty years ago, the tree was cut and the Eagles then moved to a giant pine near the edge of the marsh. Here for over thirty years their nest was located until the hurricane of August 22, 1933, came sweeping across the marsh and tore the great nest from its place. The nest was not in use when destroyed, in fact no attempt had been made to rear a brood there for three years. A local egg collector had paid it yearly visits until the Eagles ceased to breed there. They still guarded the tree, however, for in 1933 they routed a pair of Ospreys that attempted to nest on the top of the old nest.

Fig. 23. A bald eagle nest with young in a loblolly pine at the Blackwater National Wildlife Refuge, May 20, 1976.

Fig. 24. An adult bald eagle alighting on a nest located at the Blackwater National Wildlife Refuge in the spring of 1976. Photograph by William H. Julian, U.S. Fish and Wildlife Service.

"The remains of the nest were carefully sifted by hand and placed in baskets for weighing. All food remains were carefully saved. For this work Mr. Peter J. Van Huizen, acting supervisor of Blackwater Migratory Bird Refuge, gave valuable assistance. The forty-three bushels of material in the nest weighed 1,274 pounds."

Smith estimated that when the nest was in use it must have weighed a ton. In falling during the storm, some of the nest material may have been scattered and irretrievable. From observations made from the ground when the nest tree was still standing, it appeared to Smith that the nest was over ten feet in depth and from four to five feet across at the top. Whether the same pair used the Gum Swamp nest for 30 years is a matter of conjecture. It is known that captive bald eagles have lived for 35 years.

Fig. 25. Bald eagle flying from nest in Virginia pine, Arnold, Anne Arundel County, Maryland, February 1936.

J. Warren Jacobs, writing in Bent (11), describes a huge nest in Florida that measured 15 feet in depth and eight feet across. In addition to the giant size, it was unique in having an eagle incubating a set of eggs on the top of the great pile and a great horned owl incubating two eggs in a cavity in the side of the nest, four feet from the bottom of the pile!

Nests are constructed mostly of sticks, with a few clumps of sod, cornstalks (occasionally with ears attached), and if near a marsh, a few cattail stalks. In the Blackwater country nests are usually lined with marsh grass. As material is added year after year, the core of the nest comes to form a sodden mass of vegetable mold. Sticks up to six feet in length have been noted in eagle nests. Many odd items were found in the nest described by Smith, including acorns and periwinkle snails (neither used for food), furnace clinkers, and muskrat traps.

Through the years fragments of nonedible food, the bones of muskrats, feet of ducks, heads of fish, skulls of birds, and other items, filter down into the interstices of a nest. Smith (10) lists the remains of animals found in the Gum Swamp nest: muskrat 35; waterfowl 8; fish, several; spotted turtle 1; blue crab 1; and part of what appeared to be the skull of a red-tailed hawk. From this list, as Smith points out, the eagles at the Gum Swamp nest depended mostly on the marsh for food. The hawk was the only victim not directly associated with the marsh. However, red-tailed hawks commonly hunt over the Blackwater marsh and feed on some of the same animals as eagles.

Some of the muskrats probably were taken from traps, but it is the opinion of Smith and other biologists studying muskrats that most of the rats were picked up dead on the marsh. Eagles, like vultures and some of the hawks, also feed on carrion. Most of the ducks taken were shot by hunters. One of the waterfowl breastbones from the nest had two shot holes in it.

In a publication by Imler and Kalmbach (12), the authors present additional data on the food preferences of bald eagles at Blackwater. These data are based on regurgitated pellets collected by Frank Smith during the period March 1933 to March 1934. Smith apparently obtained the pellets at nests, beneath nest trees, and beneath a feeding station, usually a dead tree out in the marsh. This information is presented in detail (Table 1), but as Imler and Kalmbach state . . .

"it is important to point out that pellet material alone tends to minimize the recording of fish which the eagles may have eaten to the exclusion of animals clothed in fur or feathers. Many of the smaller fish bones are completely digested in the eagle's stomach and, without a binding material, the bones of fishes eaten are likely to be scattered when regurgitated and no definite pellet formed. Accordingly, it is safe to assume that the amount of fish eaten by Chesapeake Bay eagles was somewhat greater than that indicated."

While fish constituted only 4.2 percent of the proportion of food taken in this sample, in a sample of food remains taken at a number of Chesapeake Bay eagle nests in the spring months of 1936 and 1937 by W.B. Tyrell, fish comprised 52.4 percent of all foods taken (12).

From a survey of the ornithological literature, there is no doubt that, nationwide, fish furnish the eagle's main food supply. While eagles are good fishermen, they are also good scavengers, and many dead fish are taken.

Their method of fishing is quite different from the ospreys'. Ospreys usually plunge into the water from considerable heights, while eagles fly along close to the surface simply extending their feet into the water to grasp fish with their talons (Fig. 26).

The location of the nest governs to some degree the character of food fed to the young. At a nest on Lake Erie near Vermilion, Ohio, professor Herrick, writing in Bent (11), reported that in 1922, fish formed 70 percent of the food fed to the young; and in 1923, fish made up 96 percent of their food.

In the spring of 1974, an active nest was located close to the Little Blackwater River. In May of that spring it appeared to me that the adults were feeding their one eaglet mostly on fish. The eagles would perch on a snag located on a small island in

TABLE 1

An Analysis of 59 Pellets of Bald Eagles Collected at Blackwater Refuge, Maryland, March 1933 to March 1934

Food item	Occurrence Number	Occurrence Percent
FISHES:		
Gizzard shad *(Dorosoma cepedianum)*	1	--------
Fresh-water eel *(Anguilla rostrata)*	2	--------
Toadfish *(Opsanus tau)*	1	--------
Unidentified fishes	2	--------
Total	6	4.2
BIRDS:		
Pied-billed grebe *(Podilymbus podiceps)*	2	--------
Atlantic brant *(Branta bernicla)*	1	--------
Common mallard *(Anas platyrhynchos)*	4	--------
Pintail *(Anas acuta)*	3	--------
Green-winged teal *(Anas carolinensis)*	4	--------
Unidentified *Anas*	5	--------
Baldpate *(Mareca americana)*	3	--------
Wood duck *(Aix sponsa)*	1	--------
Canvasback *(Aythya valisineria)*	2	--------
Unidentified *Aythya*	7	--------
Ruddy duck *(Oxyura jamaicensis)*	1	--------
Hooded merganser *(Lophodytes cucullatus)*	1	--------
Unidentified merganser	1	--------
Unidentified ducks	17	--------
Unidentified gallinaceous birds	2	--------
Domestic chicken	9	--------
Domestic pigeon	1	--------
Unidentified birds	6	--------
Unidentified bird's egg	1	--------
Total	71	50.4
MAMMALS:		
Unidentified shrew	1	--------
Muskrat *(Ondatra zibethicus)*	29	--------
Meadow mouse *(Microtus)*	1	--------
Cottontail rabbit *(Sylvilagus floridanus)*	5	--------
Wool of domestic sheep	6	--------
Total	42	29.8
REPTILES:		
Racer *(Coluber)*	1	--------
Unidentified snakes	2	--------
Total	3	2.1
CRUSTACEANS:		
Edible crab *(Callinectes)*	1	0.7
VEGETABLE MATTER:		
Kernels of corn	8	--------
Vegetable debris	10	--------
Total	18	12.4

Fig. 26. Bald eagle fishing. Unlike the osprey which plunges from a considerable height into the water after its prey, the eagle flies along just above the water, extending its talons to grab a fish that is close to the surface. From illustration by L.A. Fuertes, courtesy of the U.S. Fish and Wildlife Service.

the river from which they swooped down over the water to catch carp that they carried to the nest.

The young eagle left the nest in June, the end of a long nesting season for the parents that had started building the nest close to a good fishing spot in December.

It is appropriate to end this narrative with the encouraging note that in 1976, the four eagle nests located on the Blackwater National Wildlife Refuge produced five young.

Tidemarsh Muskrats

Blackwater's muskrats are known to the mammalogist as the coastal or Virginia muskrat, and have been given the scientific name *Ondatra zibethicus*. According to Lowery (13), the generic name *Ondatra* is a French Canadian word of Huron Indian origin; the specific name *zibethicus* means musky-odored.

The coastal or Virginia muskrat, which has two color phases, brown or red, and black, is about two feet in length, including the tail, and averages a little over two pounds in weight (Fig. 27).

Fig. 27. The muskrat is a rodent with a vertically flattened scaly tail and hind feet that are webbed at their bases. Photograph by V.B. Scheffer, U.S. Fish and Wildlife Service.

Tidemarsh Muskrats

In the Blackwater area the muskrat is associated mainly with Olney three-square sedge, the predominant marsh type. Three-square or three-cornered grass, as it is known in some localities, is a prime food, and through the years, in the course of decay, develops a subsurface peatlike soil in which muskrats can dig a system of canals and underground tunnels (Fig. 28). No other type of bottom is as good for excavation. In sandy bottoms walls cave in, and clay is difficult to excavate and makes a muddy canal which the animal apparently does not like.

In dry marshes, muskrats make surface trails that are partly concealed by the one- to two-foot-high three-square, until the marsh is burned over in the late fall or winter. Just as these surface trails are used by rails, rice rats, and other small

Fig. 28. Muskrat plunge hole leading to tunnel in Olney three-square peat marsh.

mammals as passageways through the marsh, so are the subsurface canals utilized by turtles and other amphibious animals. Frank Smith (2) states that one Curtis Insley caught 23 muskrats in Dorchester County in a trap set on the back of a snapping turtle hibernating at the bottom of a deep muskrat canal.

In addition to being used for movement in concealment about the marsh, underground canals also lead to the muskrat's house. Muskrats of the extensive marsh country like Blackwater live mostly in dome-shaped houses or lodges that may be five or six feet in diameter at the base and three or four feet in height (Figs. 29 and 30). Those that live near the shoreline sometimes live in burrows dug into banks. The entrance hole to a bank burrow is usually below the low-tide level.

Fig. 29. Muskrat house made mostly of wads of plant material dug from the marsh.

Houses are usually made from plants common in the area where the rats live. Leaves, stalks, roots, or wads of grass utilized in construction are collected about the house site. Thus a bare area surrounds the house, and in effect is a moat, so that if the marsh is burned, the house is generally protected.

Each house has several nests from which a passage leads to an escape or plunge hole. When a house is in use, the nests are lined with fresh grass, and may be damp, but not wet.

Fig. 30. Muskrat houses are sometimes built around saplings and stumps.

Fig. 31. Olney three-square marsh showing muskrat houses and bare "eatout" areas, indicating overpopulation in habitat.

According to Smith (2), Blackwater muskrats have at least two litters a year, with most of the young born from April to September. Five young to a litter is the average. Quoting from O'Neil's work on the life of the muskrat in Louisiana (14):

"Normally, when the first litter reaches sexual maturity and the second litter reaches kit stage, the first litter is evidently forceably evicted by the original pair, to mate and repeat this same process.

"In a good three-cornered grass marsh that is sparsely populated, the young pairs will build their house within 20 or 30 feet of the original house. In some instances a pair will just build an apartment connected with the original house. This is what the trappers call a "double house," and the entire group of 10 to 15 or more muskrats live and work together. However, the usual number living together in one house is a pair of old adults and two to four young.

"These colonies continue to expand until they meet with other expanding colonies, tunnelling and destroying the food supply until the muskrats denude the entire area of practically all vegetation and cut the marsh floor to a depth of 18 to 20 inches. This is what is termed a peak population and the slide toward the trough in the population curve is inevitable."

To prevent an overpopulation of rats and consequent "eatout" of their habitat (Fig. 31) and vast reduction in numbers of animals, trappers endeavor to keep a marsh "trapped" to a stable population level.

There are other limiting factors, especially predation on the young. Raccoons and foxes are the principal predators, breaking into houses seeking the kits. Muskrats feeding out on the marsh are rarely taken by predators as they are usually close enough to a plunge hole to dive out of danger down into their underground tunnels. The relatively few muskrats taken by avian predators, hawks, owls, and eagles, are mostly sick or taken from traps.

When mammalian predators such as raccoons, foxes, or mink break into a muskrat house, they may also be searching for meadow voles (mice) and rice rats that live in occupied and unoccupied muskrat lodges (15).

The number of muskrats trapped at Blackwater Refuge each year for the commercial trade has varied considerably in the nearly 45 years of trapping there. According to Van T. Harris (16), the catch has varied from approximately 1,000 to 26,000 a year. The years 1936 to 1940 were all high catch years ranging from 19,000 to 26,000 animals. During a peak population year as in 1938, five or more muskrats per acre were trapped in the Blackwater region. It is interesting that the approximately 6,000 muskrats caught in 1933, first year of Refuge trapping records, bear a similarity to the 5,000 trapped in 1976.

Presently, trappers in Maryland earn about one million dollars a year (Fig. 32). Dorchester, with about 1,000 commercial trappers, has more than any other county, and many more muskrats are trapped there than any other animal. In 1976, black pelts were worth about $5.00, and browns or reds about $4.00.

Muskrat carcasses are used for food and have been sold in markets and restaurants in Baltimore under the assumed name of marsh rabbit, and fur coats made from muskrat pelts were formerly marketed as Hudson seal.

Tidemarsh Muskrats

Fig. 32. Tony Florio, a wildlife biologist with the Delaware Game and Fish Commission, has written a poem about his friend the muskrat trapper. Tony's elderly friend is heading out to the marsh with a bundle of poles for marking his trap sites (or sets).

Oh, Ancient Man, where goest thou
On day where light bare scapes the night?
Thy bones too brittle, thy body old—How
Can thou fight Nature's wintry smite?

I'm fixin to do me some trappin, son—
And don't give me none o' your citified lip.
I'll progg till I'm dead, and still won't be done
Til my bones're the color o' my duckin gun.

A. FLORIO

The Nutria

Most Marylanders are unaware of the large, exotic rodent that occurs in the Blackwater marshes (Fig. 33). About the size of a beaver and weighing up to 20 pounds, the nutria *(Myocaster coypus)* was introduced from South America to the Louisiana coastal marshes in the 1930s. One story has it that E.A. McIlhenny, a naturalist and the manufacturer of Tabasco Sauce, who lived on Avery Island out in the Louisiana marshes, imported 20 nutria from Argentina. Several of his specimens escaped from holding pens, and now there are several million in the Gulf Coast marshes surrounding McIlhenny's home.

Herbert Dozier, who was conducting furbearing animal research for the U.S. Fish and Wildlife Service, brought them to Blackwater in the 1940s. During the winter of 1975-76, 3,200 were trapped at Blackwater. Trappers received about $3.00 per pelt. In Louisiana, where it is now the chief furbearing animal, 1,611,623 nutria were trapped for commercial purposes in the 1972-73 season.

When nutria began showing up in the Louisiana marshes, it was thought that they would compete with the smaller muskrat, causing a reduction of that valuable fur resource. Apparently there is not much competition between nutria and muskrats unless there is a scarcity of food in the marshes. According to Lowery (13), "Since

Fig. 33. The nutria is a Temperate Zone rodent from South America. It was introduced to the Louisiana Gulf Coast marshes in the 1930s, and the Blackwater marshes in the 1940s. Its center of distribution in Maryland is still in the Blackwater area where some 3,200 were trapped for the fur trade in the winter of 1975-76. Photograph by Herbert L. Dozier, U.S. Fish and Wildlife Service.

The Nutria

muskrats live mainly in different kinds of marshes, the former being primarily an animal of certain types of salt or brackish marshes, the latter of freshwater situations, direct competition between them is a concern only in a few places where both happen to be present together in large numbers."

In southern Dorchester County I generally see them in the fresher marshes along the Blackwater and Little Blackwater Rivers, the nearby Transquaking River (Fig. 34), and at Elliott Island, across Fishing Bay from Blackwater. In these areas I have seen them feeding on cattails and water lilies, mainly freshwater plants.

Apparently they do not occur in appreciable numbers elsewhere in Maryland marshes. It would seem that they would be increasing and extending their range in our tidal marshes as they are Temperate Zone animals in South America and should thus be at home in this latitude. However, severe winters like the one of 1976-77 can have a devastating effect on the nutria population.

The vernacular and other names of the nutria have, according to Lowery (13), been derived as follows: The word nutria is a Spanish cognate of the Latin word *lutra*, and these names have been applied to various aquatic mammals, including the well-known river otter. The generic name *Myocaster* is derived from two Greek words (*mys*, for mouse, and *kaster*, for beaver) that translate as mouse beaver. The specific name *coypus* is the Latinized form of coypu, a name in the language of the Araucanian Indians of south-central Chile and adjacent parts of Argentina, for an aquatic mammal that was possibly this species. Coypu is another vernacular or common name for this large South American rodent.

Fig. 34. Habitat of nutria along Transquaking River, September 1976. Vegetation in marsh is mainly Olney three-square, tidemarsh waterhemp, millet, saltmarsh cordgrass, and narrowleaf cattail. Note great egret in cove.

The Delmarva Fox Squirrel

The Delmarva fox squirrel is one of our rare North American mammals. Because of its sparse numbers and restricted distribution, it is listed as an endangered species by the U.S. Fish and Wildlife Service. There are probably less than a thousand of these rare fox squirrels. This remnant population is concentrated mainly in the Blackwater section of Dorchester County and at Eastern Neck National Wildlife Refuge in Kent County. A few were known to occur sometime during the last 50 years in other Eastern Shore counties—Queen Annes, Talbot, Wicomico, Somerset, and Worcester.

At one time the range of this endemic mammal extended from Northampton County, on the Eastern Shore of Virginia, to southeastern Pennsylvania. The Blackwater area apparently has always been the center of distribution. Approximately 300 are found there today. If it were not for the two federal wildlife refuges on the Eastern Shore, the Delmarva fox squirrel would possibly be extinct.

Fig. 35. The Delmarva fox squirrel is an Eastern Shore endemic. Its center of distribution is the Blackwater area of southern Dorchester County. It is larger and lighter in color than the gray squirrel, lives mostly in pine woods, and spends much of its time on the ground. Photograph by William H. Julian, U.S. Fish and Wildlife Service.

The Delmarva Fox Squirrel

The fox squirrel of the Eastern Shore of Maryland differs markedly in color from the Eastern fox squirrel of the Appalachians. The Delmarva variety, or subspecies, has the scientific name *Seiurus niger cinereus*, the subspecific name *cinereus* referring to its ashy-gray pelage (Fig. 35). The eastern subspecies or variety, *Seiurus niger vulpinus*, is a brownish rufescence in color, the subspecific name *vulpinus* referring to the technical generic name of the red fox *(Vulpes fulva)*.

The Delmarva fox squirrel somewhat resembles the common eastern gray squirrel, but is lighter and considerably larger (see Fig. 36). One who is familiar with both species has little difficulty in distinguishing between the two. The Delmarva is shyer, slower and more deliberate, and essentially a piney-woods squirrel, although it occurs in mixed pine-hardwoods stands, and occasionally in pure hardwoods.

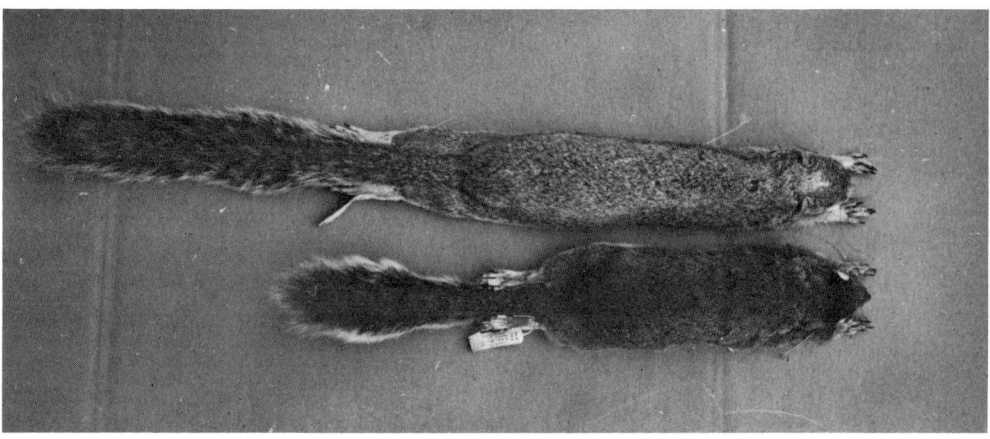

Fig. 36. Museum study skins illustrating difference in size of Delmarva fox squirrel (top) and gray squirrel.

In May 1974, I spent several days observing Delmarvas along the edge of an open field next to their home woods to find out if they pulled up sprouting corn. I was interested in conducting an experiment with a special chemical seed treatment to prevent sprout-pulling by blackbirds, particularly common grackles. It didn't take long to discover that fox squirrels do, indeed, love corn, and even though the candidate seed treatment had a very low mammalian toxicity, we couldn't take chances and had to move our experiment to Pungo National Wildlife Refuge in eastern North Carolina where there were no rare animals at that season.

The fox squirrels that I observed along the edge of a sprouting cornfield adjacent to Blackwater Refuge land, were seldom more than two or three feet from the woods. There were often six or eight of them out in the open feeding at one time. The farmer, realizing that the squirrels would be digging up the sprouts to get at the kernels, had strung out a line of seed corn for about 200 feet along the edge of the field to serve as a buffer so that the squirrels would not pull up the sprouts. This deterrent seemed to work very well, as very few sprouts had been dug out. The woods bordering the field was typical Delmarva fox squirrel habitat—a mature to

Fig. 37. Bill Geise (left) and Guy Willey, of the Blackwater Refuge staff, standing next to mature loblolly pine in typical fox squirrel habitat at Blackwater, April 1976.

overripe mixed loblolly pine-hardwoods stand with some of the pines over 100 years old (Fig. 37). Another aspect of this optimum stand was the open understory, a feature usually associated with mature forests which have characteristically heavy or dense canopies through which little sunlight can penetrate.

Fox squirrels spend more time on the ground foraging than grays, and like wild turkeys, which also favor mature forests with an open understory, have to have an

The Delmarva Fox Squirrel

extended view of their surroundings so that they can retreat when threatened. Part of the management program at Blackwater Refuge is to burn the understory of the piney woods to keep it devoid of shrubs and saplings.

These older forests usually produce an abundance of pine mast or seed, a staple food of fox squirrels, and their presence in a pine woods can usually be detected by the piles of chipped-off scales and cores of pine cones at the base of a pine tree (Fig. 38).

Fig. 38. Scales and cores of pine cones are frequently found at the base of a pine tree indicating that a Delmarva fox squirrel has been feeding on one of its favorite foods, pine seed.

Like other squirrels, they feed on a variety of foods, including corn in the roasting-ear stage, soybeans, and walnuts. Guy Willey, of the Refuge staff, states that in early spring he has observed them feeding on the fruit or "keys" of the red maple. In the autumn of 1976, I saw a number of walnuts, some partly eaten, in a fox squirrel woods. Yet, there were no walnut trees in that woods; the nearest trees were a quarter of a mile away.

Although the fox squirrel is partial to pine woods, and the gray to hardwoods, I have seen mixed pine-hardwoods stands at Blackwater where both squirrels get along harmoniously. I have seen them feeding 20 feet apart. When I approached them, the gray would immediately take to a tree, while the fox would run a long way on the ground before climbing a tree or would just disappear from view while still running along through the forest.

Fig. 39. A fox squirrel nest far out on the limb of a loblolly pine, and about 40 feet from the ground. Nests are made mostly of pine branches and needles, and sometimes with plants brought up from a nearby marsh.

Unlike the gray squirrel, that usually builds its nest in the crotch of a tree, the Delmarva's nest is well out on a limb (Fig. 39). Nests that I have seen at Blackwater were made mostly of pine twigs with needles attached. If the woods was next to a marsh, some dried marsh plants, such as cattail stalks, were incorporated into the nest structure.

There are several hundred acres of mature pine woods at Blackwater National Wildlife Refuge. This wooded area and the protection that goes along with it insures the perpetuation of this rare animal, barring a catastrophe such as disease.

Breeding Birds of the Loblolly Pine Woods

The piney woods along with the marshes of southern Dorchester County are a dominating feature of the landscape. Loblolly pine, a southern tree that reaches its northern limit in southern Delaware, is extended northward into the Delmarva Peninsula because of the moderating influence of the Gulf Stream and the sandy Coastal Plain soils. Of the eight species of southern pines, the loblolly has the widest site tolerance. In the Blackwater area it grows on relatively dry sites often mixed with hardwoods, and in pure stands that sometimes extend a short distance into the marshes. Thus, in some sections loblolly pines are growing in damp soil or standing water much of the time. As the pines extend into the marshes the stand tends to thin out and some of the pines succumb to saturation, thus leaving a number of dead stumps. The combination of live pines and dead stumps (Fig. 40) generally supports a greater variety of nesting birds than the denser part of a stand farther inland from

Fig. 40. Live pines and dead pine stumps standing a short distance out in Blackwater marsh. Old woodpecker holes and natural cavities in dead stumps are used for nesting by brown-headed nuthatches, house wrens, crested flycatchers, tree swallows, Carolina chickadees, tufted titmice, and bluebirds. A kingbird and a yellow warbler had nests in the live pines shown in this photograph. Much of the kingbird's nest was made of the soft downy material from cattails.

the marsh (Fig. 41). Woodpeckers nest in the dead stumps, and brown-headed nuthatches, bluebirds, house wrens, Carolina chickadees, crested flycatchers, and tree swallows (Figs. 42 and 43) utilize old woodpecker holes and natural cavities for nesting.

Fig. 41. Mature loblolly pine forest, southern Dorchester County. Understory is mainly wax myrtle and American holly. Nesting habitat of chuck-will's-widow, brown-headed nuthatch, red-cockaded woodpecker, pine warbler, fish crow, great horned owl, and several other species of birds.

The avifauna of the maritime loblolly pine forest of Dorchester County is represented by three species of southern birds, the chuck-will's-widow (Fig. 44), the brown-headed nuthatch (Fig. 45), and the red-cockaded woodpecker (see Fig. 50). The chuck-will's and the nuthatch reach their northern limit with the loblolly pines in southern Delaware, and the red-cockaded woodpecker in southern Dorchester County.

Fig. 42. This pine stub is eight feet tall and six inches in diameter, and on May 13, 1977, one of its three old woodpecker holes was occupied by a nesting tree swallow, another by a nesting brown-headed nuthatch, and a third by a flying squirrel. Note tree swallow perched on limb near top of stub on left. Blackwater National Wildlife Refuge.

Fig. 43. Tree swallow perched at entrance to nest in dead pine stub located in the Blackwater marsh, May 28, 1977. The nest was lined with an assortment of feathers taken from the marsh, and included those of Canada goose, mallard, and green-winged teal. Photograph by Mike Haramis, U.S. Fish and Wildlife Service.

Fig. 44. Chuck-will's-widow, a southern nesting bird of the maritime loblolly pine forest, reaches its northern limit on the Delmarva Peninsula. Illustration by John W. Taylor.

Fig. 45. Brown-headed nuthatch at nest hole in pine, bringing grasshopper to nestlings. This southern nuthatch reaches its northern limit on the Delmarva Peninsula. Photograph by S.A. Grimes.

The variety and relative abundance of birds that nest in the loblolly pine woods habitat in the Blackwater area is indicated by a census that I made of territorial males during a two-hour period on May 20, 1976: pine warbler 12, rufous-sided towhee 7, house wren 6, flicker 6, crested flycatcher 6, brown-headed nuthatch 5, blue-gray gnatcatcher 5, yellowthroat 4, wood pewee 4, Carolina wren 3, cardinal 3, red-bellied woodpecker 2, wood thrush 2, summer tanager 2, mourning dove 2, brown-headed cowbird 2, blue jay 2, white-eyed vireo 2, bluebird 2, tufted titmouse 1, red-tailed hawk 1, bald eagle 1 (active nest), great horned owl 1, ovenbird 1, Carolina chickadee 1, hairy woodpecker 1, pileated woodpecker 1, and red-headed woodpecker 1. Several local pine woods species were not encountered when the census was made. Among those missed were the fish crow, chuck-will's-widow, and yellow-throated warbler. Of special interest was the red-headed woodpecker, now a rare nesting bird in the Blackwater area as well as most of the eastern half of Maryland. Also, only three have been seen on southern Dorchester Christmas bird counts in 30 years.

Several species listed in the foregoing paragraph are associated with the understory shrubs, saplings, ferns, marshy vegetation, or other ground cover of the pine

Fig. 46. Eggs of chuck-will's-widow at "nest" site on ground in mature loblolly pine forest approximately three miles south of the Blackwater River, May 25, 1959. The eggs were placed on the pine straw with not even a slight depression for a nest. Two newly hatched chicks were found near this same site on June 18, 1958.

Breeding Birds of the Loblolly Pine Woods

woods, and would include the white-eyed vireo, ovenbird, yellowthroat, and towhee. The towhee and ovenbird do most of their feeding on the ground, and nest there, as does the chuck-will's-widow (Fig. 46). As also mentioned, many of the pine woods birds are hole nesters that utilize dead stubs or stumps. An interesting example is the crested flycatcher, a bird about the size of a cardinal. The crested uses an old woodpecker hole or natural cavity in a dead pine and usually lines its nest with a cast-off snakeskin. Wood ducks use old nest holes excavated by pileated woodpeckers in dead or dying pines. I noted that one of these ducks was incubating a clutch of eggs in one such abandoned woodpecker hole at Blackwater on April 1, 1976.

Fig. 47. An adult great horned owl, denizen of pine woods and mixed pine-hardwoods in the Blackwater region. The horned owl is the earliest nesting bird in the area. Ralph Jackson found a nest with eggs as early as January 27 (1923). Photograph by John Hamlet.

Fig. 48. Young great horned owl that has recently left the nest. Horned owls use abandoned nests of red-tailed hawks, crows, or bald eagles. Active nests that I have examined contained remains of rabbits, squirrels, meadow voles, and towhees.

Yellow warblers occasionally nest in pines along the edge of a woods. Bill Julian showed me the fallen nest of one of these birds. It appeared to be made mostly of the hair of some mammal that I could not identify on the spot, but also included some feathers of a king rail. Some years earlier I had watched a yellow-throated warbler, another bird that nests in pines, gathering hair for the lining of its nest from the carcass of a deer lying a hundred feet or so from the nest site.

The nesting season in the loblolly pine forest is extended from late January into September, with most species nesting within the period April-June. The earliest nesting bird is the great horned owl (Figs. 47 and 48) which usually selects a last-year's red-tailed hawk nest in which to lay its eggs. Ralph Jackson, the Cambridge ornithologist, examined 20 nests of horned owls in Dorchester County and

Breeding Birds of the Loblolly Pine Woods

Fig. 49. Nest of mourning dove on charred pine stump. Doves usually place their nests on limbs or in a crotch of a tree, but occasionally on the ground. The nesting season is a long one, and in Maryland, doves are nesting at some time between January and October.

found the earliest with a complete set of two eggs on January 27, 1923. The bald eagle, which builds its nest in pine trees in this area, usually lays its eggs in February. Jackson's earliest date for fresh eggs in eight nests examined is February 21, 1924.

Mourning doves have the longest nesting season of the pine woods birds, with pairs nesting some time between February and September. I found a nest in another Maryland county with large young in February, and backdating, the eggs would have to have been laid in January. Doves usually nest on a pine bough, in the crotch of a tree, or occasionally on the ground. One nest that I found was located in the depression of a charred pine stump (Fig. 49). Doves also nest in hardwoods, ornamentals, and even other sites. Certainly the pine woods has an advantage over other forest types for early nesting species like the great horned owl and mourning dove, as its foliage endures throughout all seasons.

On the Trail of the Red-Cockaded Woodpecker

The red-cockaded woodpecker is the rarest bird in Maryland, where it reaches its northern limit in the eastern United States. In this state, it is known to occur presently only in the Blackwater area (Fig. 50). Most of the timber on the Blackwater Refuge is loblolly pine; some of it is overripe or overmature, and that is what red-cockades require. They nest only in pines that are 70 years old or older, and that are infected with redheart, a fungus disease that softens the heartwood and makes excavation of the nest easy. Some of Blackwater's pines are over a hundred years old, and in my travels throughout the southern range of the red-cockade, I have never seen a more suitable habitat.

Fig. 50. Red-cockaded woodpecker at nest in live pine. White face patch and ladderback markings identify this southern woodpecker. Photograph by William H. Julian, U.S. Fish and Wildlife Service.

The history of the occurrence of the red-cockaded woodpecker in Maryland is indeed interesting and has mostly been centered in the Blackwater region. It was discovered at Blackwater on June 2, 1932, by Frank Smith, a biologist working at the Refuge. The next sighting was of a bird I saw in the pines at Assateague Island on June 9, 1939. It was then unreported in the state until 1955, when Mr. P. Hurlock saw one in the Golden Hill area a few miles southwest of Blackwater Refuge on October 8, 1955 (4). Several pairs were seen in the Golden Hill tract, and an active nest was found there by Robert E. Stewart and me on May 30, 1958 (Fig. 51). This well-known red-cockaded woodpecker tract was lumbered in the early 1960s, and the birds' whereabouts then became unknown.

Fig. 51. The only active nest of a red-cockaded woodpecker ever found in Maryland. This nest was located about three miles southwest of the Blackwater National Wildlife Refuge on May 30, 1958.

Matthew C. Perry and I then watched a pair for two hours in the central part of the State near Bowie, Prince Georges County, on May 11, 1974. The pair were feeding in a stand of mature Virginia and shortleaf pines; but evidently were simply wandering, as they were not seen again. Identifiable photographs were made of one of the birds. These birds were somewhat north of their normal range. Then it was back to Blackwater Refuge, where Guy Willey, Refuge Biologist, saw three on March 26, 1976.

It seems logical to think that a few of these woodpeckers may have been at Blackwater all along, since the habitat is optimum for them. Yet, a Christmas count involving many persons has been conducted at the Refuge each winter for nearly 30 years, and only once has a red-cockade been recorded. If they were there, sooner or later they would be seen because red-cockades are noisy, maintaining a constant chatter for extended periods; and unlike other woodpeckers, usually occur in small groups with several of them calling at one time; and they are less suspicious than other woodpeckers and can be more closely approached.

The day before Guy Willey saw the red-cockades in March 1976, he took me into the area where he thought they might occur. The loblolly tract (Fig. 52) was located next to a marsh and the ground was wet. In the wetter sections the marsh had invaded the piney woods and the ground cover was composed of sedges, rushes, switchgrass, and other marsh plants. Other woodpeckers seen in the area were the downy, hairy, red-bellied, pileated, and the flicker.

During our search we became more aware of the fact that the pileated woodpecker, a bird nearly the size of a crow, also is attracted to live but deteriorating pine trees, chiseling rectangular-shaped holes in search of insects (Fig. 53).

Nest holes of red-cockaded woodpeckers that have been in use for some time are easy to spot as they are surrounded by an extensive area of whitish resin. Most of the whitish area of pitch or resin is beneath the hole, but sometimes surrounds it. The exuding resin is due to the work of the woodpecker in drilling many small holes in the cambium layer of the pine in the area of the nest hole. It is believed that this is done for the purpose of discouraging other birds, flying squirrels, snakes, and ants from entering the nest cavity. Most trees in which nests occur usually look as much alive as healthy trees, and the birds will continue to use them until the sap no longer oozes.

Because of its highly specialized nesting requirements, the red-cockade is becoming a rare bird in many parts of its range. The old diseased and dying pines required for nesting are being culled by foresters. Modern forestry practices call for harvesting trees on a 25-30-year cycle for pulp and up to 60 years for pole or saw timber, long before they reach the stage when they can be utilized by the woodpecker. But there is hope for the red-cockade, as the plight of the bird has come to the attention of the conservationist, and measures are being taken to preserve nest trees in some areas. Some of the large commercial lumber interests are cooperating in this venture, and there will probably always be a scattering of overmature pines

Fig. 52. Guy Willey (left) and Bill Julian, of the Blackwater Refuge staff, searching for red-cockaded woodpeckers, April 1976.

on large southern estates and in sanctuaries and national forests where this extremely selective bird can find nesting trees to meet its requirements. Blackwater is one of those places where a small population can probably be perpetuated.

The nearest populations to Blackwater's are in southeastern Virginia, near Suffolk, Wakefield, and Franklin.

Fig. 53. Rectangular excavations in overmature loblolly pine are typical work of pileated woodpecker searching for woodboring insects. Blackwater National Wildlife Refuge.

The Timberdoodle

"Secretive, solitary and abroad chiefly in the dim light of dusk and dawn it remains to most obscure and unknown." This is the timberdoodle or woodcock (Fig. 54), as so well described by John Taylor, the artist, in *Virginia Wildlife* (17). Timberdoodle is the name applied by some of the old-time Maryland hunters. Naturalists and hunters know this shy bird. Hunters are intrigued by the zig-zag target whirring through a boggy thicket, and naturalists are interested in the sky dance it performs at twilight during the courtship period in early spring. To see one at any other time, you almost have to step on it. When flushing it underfoot, it takes off in a twisting flight with a vibrating whistle that comes from air rushing through the three narrow outer primary feathers of the wing.

Woodcock occur at Blackwater at all seasons, with low numbers in the winter. They prefer the damp pine woods and hardwood swamps. I often flush them in old-growth pine woods when looking for the rare red-cockaded woodpecker.

Fig. 54. Woodcock or timberdoodle, and chicks. Photograph was made by Peter J. Van Huizen at the Blackwater National Wildlife Refuge in the early 1930s. Photograph courtesy of U.S. Fish and Wildlife Service.

They feed during the day or night, probing in the soft earth with their long bills for earthworms and other organisms. In Louisiana, where I lived for several years and on occasion banded woodcock at night during the winter, we usually captured our birds with mist nets in pasturelands bordering a swamp. They remained under cover of the swamp during the day.

A section of an open field near a woods margin or an opening in a thicket is the courtship and mating place when the birds arrive on the breeding grounds in late winter or early spring. Woodcock are among the earliest migrants to arrive from the South. Some have returned to Maryland nesting grounds by mid-February.

When the male woodcock returns to its breeding area, it stakes out a singing ground from which it performs its mating ritual night after night. William G. Sheldon, author of the *Book of the American Woodcock* (18), calls the courtship sky dance of the male woodcock ". . . one of the most remarkable performances in the avian world . . . " It begins its courtship call at about dusk or shortly thereafter. *Peenting* is the term used by most authors to describe the courtship calling. But to some of us, a drawn-out *beep* sounds more appropriate than *peent*. The beep or peent, which sounds much like the call of a nighthawk, is given from the ground preceding the sky dance. As many as 50 or more beeps or peents may be uttered before the male woodcock ascends skyward. Sheldon's report on the performance of a typical male follows:

"After 158 peents, occupying five minutes, our bird flushes, quickly rising on a gradual plane until we see him against the twilight sky. Fifty feet above his departure point on the ground the accelerating wing beats create a musical twitter. At first in wide circles that encompass three acres, he rises higher and higher in ever-smaller circles or ellipses until he appears batlike 275 feet above us. Briefly the twittering of wings stops, and he appears virtually to hover as he pours forth his true song—a variable series of liquid chirps, which he repeats several times as he glides to the ground on a zig-zag course. He lands close to the same spot from which he had launched himself a minute before."

After repeating his peents or beeps for several minutes from the ground, he again soars skyward.

Although the nest of the female may be several hundred feet from the peenting or beeping spot, the male's aerial flight often carries it over the incubating bird. The female visits the male's singing ground for mating.

The courtship performance or spring rites of the male woodcock are generally performed during the first hour after dusk, but occasionally for a short period before dawn; and on moonlight nights, well through the evening. In some areas the singing fields may be close enough to each other so that two or three woodcock may be heard at one time.

Nests are mere depressions on the ground in the woods (Fig. 55). Earliest nests in Maryland have been noted by the last week in February; but a nest that I found on March 21, 1976, is more of an average date. The incubating bird sits very close and can usually be touched or even picked up from the nest (Fig. 56). A sitting bird is so well camouflaged that unless its nest is near the trail of a predatory animal, it usually

The Timberdoodle

Fig. 55. Woodcock nest—a mere depression in the leaves. Four eggs are a normal clutch.

escapes detection. Snakes have been known to take the eggs, as P.J. Van Huizen found an egg in a black snake at Blackwater Refuge. The precocial young leave the nest within an hour or so after hatching (Fig. 57).

Local woodcock remain through the summer and begin migrating south in September and October to wintering grounds in the Southeastern States. The main transient migration is in November. The peak southward flight at Blackwater in the fall of 1976 seemed to be on November 19, when I saw many flying across the road as I drove along at dusk. Some late migrants from farther north that have remained behind because of warm weather, are still passing through in December.

Each winter some woodcock are noted on the annual Christmas count conducted in southern Dorchester County. During counts made on December 26, 1972, December 26, 1973, and December 30, 1974, 25, 19, and 16, respectively, were seen.

Since much of the land in southern Dorchester County is soggy and seldom freezes until later in the winter, some woodcock that have come from farther north are likely to remain there as long as they can probe in the soil. Records indicate that the latitude of southern Dorchester County is about the northern limit for an appreciable number of wintering woodcock.

Fig. 56. Woodcock on nest, March 23, 1976.

Fig. 57. Woodcock chick found in April 1976, and photographed by Matthew C. Perry, U.S. Fish and Wildlife Service.

The Atlantic Blue-Winged Teal

In an article appearing in the 1932 *Auk* (19), journal of the American Ornithologists' Union, Oliver Austin of the U.S. Biological Survey reported the first evidence of the nesting of the blue-winged teal in Maryland. Austin's report was based on information obtained in the Blackwater marshes in the period 1929-31. This proved to be an interesting discovery as this small species of waterfowl was thought to be only a spring and fall migrant and occasional winter visitor in the Chesapeake Bay Country, with breeding populations originating mainly in the pothole region of the northern prairie states and Prairie Provinces of Canada (particularly Saskatchewan and Manitoba).

Austin recorded the events leading to the discovery of the young and nests of the blue-winged teal at Blackwater: On July 13, 1929, W.G. Tregoe of Cambridge, a warden with the Maryland Game and Inland Fish Commission, found several young ducks that he believed were teal, and whose identification was later confirmed by Talbot Denmead, ornithologist with the U.S. Biological Survey; and while canoeing on the Blackwater and Little Blackwater Rivers in June and July 1930, Denmead observed several broods of blue-winged teal; then on May 27, 1931, Austin, Tregoe, and others found the first nest and eggs. The nest was located about 200 yards from Shorter's Landing.

At the time of the Blackwater discovery a small population was known to nest in the Louisiana Gulf Coastal marshes, and now it was established that a breeding population also existed in the Dorchester County marshes. It is interesting to note that the blue-winged teal no longer nests in Louisiana.

Some years later, in the early 1950s, Robert E. Stewart and John W. Aldrich, ornithologists with the U.S. Fish and Wildlife Service, suspecting that the Chesapeake Bay birds might be morphologically different enough from western or interior breeding populations of blue-winged teal to be a distinct subspecies, collected a series of breeding specimens from Dorchester marshes in May, June, and July. Upon comparing them with museum specimens of breeding birds from the interior, it became apparent that Dorchester County specimens were much darker than those from the Midwest and Prairie Provinces of Canada. In the course of their examinations of many specimens from several museums, they found that all breeding blue-winged teal from the Atlantic Coastal region extending from North Carolina to the Maritime Provinces of Canada were much darker than birds from the interior. So, as Stewart and Aldrich state in their published paper on the subject (20), "It is concluded on the basis of marked color differences and apparent geographical segregation during the breeding season that two recognizable races of blue-winged teal exist which are sufficiently distinct to warrant application of different subspecific names." Thus, the authors described and named their new geographic race or subspecies *Anas discors orphna*, the Atlantic blue-winged teal. The interior subspecies then became known as *Anas discors discors*. The technical terms have the following meanings: *Anas* is Latin for duck; *discors* is Latin for discordant, a reference to the sound made when teal take off in flight; and *orphna* is from the Greek *orphnos*, meaning dark or dusky.

The authors indicate that the center of abundance of the Atlantic blue-winged teal breeding population is in the brackish tidal marshes of New Jersey, Delaware, and Maryland, particularly in Dorchester County, Maryland, and Delaware Bay marshes of Delaware and New Jersey.

Since the study of speciation and subspeciation in birds is often of little interest or is unknown to the layman, it should be pointed out that many of our species of birds are separated into subspecies or geographic races by ornithologists on the basis of size or color differences, or both. As taxonomic studies of birds continue, museum or university scientists find that some species cannot be separated only into distinct races or subspecies, as in the case of the blue-winged teal, but that some can be lumped into a single species. A good example of lumping is our Baltimore oriole, which until 1973 was considered to be a distinct species. But it was found that its western counterpart, Bullock's oriole, intergrades with the Baltimore in the Great Plains States; thus, the two subspecies have been lumped into a single species known as the northern oriole. So in this case, instead of having two species of orioles, there are now two subspecies which differ from each other only slightly in plumage markings.

The most obvious examples of subspecies regularly occurring in the Chesapeake Bay Country are the purple and bronzed grackles. Our native grackle is the purple; the bronzed nests in New England and west of the Appalachians from the Gulf Coast to northern Canada. Both subspecies occur together in the Chesapeake region in the winter and during migration. The bronzed-backed birds and the purple-backed birds are quite distinct, especially the males, but as in the case of the orioles just mentioned, they interbreed where their ranges overlap.

The study of speciation and subspeciation of birds is a fascinating science, and as pursued by several of our Maryland ornithologists, has resulted in an interesting and significant contribution to North American ornithology.

Breeding Birds of Blackwater Marshes

On its Blackwater breeding grounds, the blue-winged teal is mainly associated with the saltmarsh meadow, placing its nest in the short, dense saltmeadow cordgrass (Fig. 58). Most species of brackish marsh nesting birds at Blackwater are found in this habitat. The saltmarsh meadow is a little higher and drier than the extensive Olney three-square, narrowleaf cattail, or needlerush plant communities.

Fig. 58. Blue-winged teal nest and eggs in brackish marsh composed of salt grass and saltmeadow cordgrass, Dorchester County, May.

Following a winter burn, the new growth of Olney three-square in the spring is less dense and apparently too tall for some brackish marsh nesting species of birds. Where there is a mixture of old growth missed by the winter burn and new growth, such thicker patches are the most important nesting sites for the Virginia rail, and are as important to nesting red-winged blackbirds as are the clumps or tufts of grass in the saltmeadow.

Fig. 59. A seaside sparrow singing its primary advertising song from a favorite territorial perch in brackish needlerush marsh.

Fig. 60. Nest and eggs of seaside sparrow in marsh mixture of saltmarsh cordgrass and saltmeadow cordgrass.

Breeding Birds of Blackwater Marshes

The three most abundant breeding birds of Blackwater's extensive marshlands are the seaside sparrow (Fig. 59), nesting mainly in the saltmarsh meadow (Fig. 60), the long-billed marsh wren, which nests in Olney three-square (Fig. 61) and taller plants, and the red-winged blackbird (Fig. 62) that nests in saltmarsh meadow, Olney three-square, cattails, and shrubs bordering marshes and tidal guts (Figs. 63 and 64).

Fig. 61. Long-billed marsh wren nest (center of photo) in stand of Olney three-square, Blackwater River marsh, June 23, 1976.

The black duck is the breeding bird most closely identified with Blackwater marshes because it is fairly common, highly visible, and is an important game species (Figs. 65 and 66). While many black duck nests at Blackwater are located in the saltmarsh meadow, a variety of sites may also be used, including the brush-covered roof of a duck blind, a dry scrubby field (Fig. 67), and often vegetation bordering a tidal gut (Fig. 68). The nesting season for the black duck is a long one. Vern Stotts and David E. Davis (21) reported nesting as early as March 9, and Ralph Jackson (1), as late as August 24.

Fig. 62. Female red-winged blackbird with food for nestlings. The redwing is the most abundant nesting bird of Chesapeake Bay marshes. It nests in grasses, sedges, rushes, shrubs, and saplings. In one area I found nests in 72 species of plants.

Fig. 63. Well concealed nest of red-winged blackbird in clump of cordgrass, with an enlargement inset to show eggs, June 1960.

Fig. 64. Nest of red-winged blackbird constructed mostly of eelgrass. Eelgrass is a submerged aquatic plant that drifts ashore when it dies. The female redwing would have obtained the dried plants from a windrow at the edge of the water.

Fig. 65. Young black ducks in tidal gut. Shrubby vegetation in background is high-tide bush.

Fig. 66. Portrait of a black duckling. Photograph by Matthew C. Perry, U.S. Fish and Wildlife Service.

Fig. 67. Black ducks nest in a variety of sites. Sam George points to a nest placed under a small pine, a half mile from a creek.

Fig. 68. This black duck nest in a stand of big cordgrass was ten feet from a tidal creek.

The black duck is persistent in its efforts to reproduce. In 1954, Vern Stotts (22) banded two females which he trapped while they were on their nests. Both nests were later destroyed by crows, but within three weeks each had constructed another nest within 100 yards of the old site. It is of interest to note further that two years later both females nested within a few yards of their 1954 nests.

Fig. 69. Adult black rail. This species of rail is about the size of a sparrow, and is normally the most secretive bird in North America; but it is readily attracted to its tape-recorded call. It can sometimes be caught by hand as it wanders up to the tape recorder.

While the black duck is one of the best-known breeding birds of the Blackwater marsh, the black rail is one of the least known (Fig. 69). This secretive little rail, the size of a sparrow, is fairly common across Fishing Bay at Elliott Island. One can stop along the road that winds through the marsh toward the village of Elliott and hear a number of them after about 9:00 p.m. on most nights in May and June. But one seldom hears a black rail along the Shorter's Wharf road that runs through the saltmeadow habitat at Blackwater. However, since the habitat extends for several miles east of Shorter's Wharf road in the direction of Fishing Bay, it is possible that a sizable breeding population occurs in this "uncharted" (by ornithologists) section of the Blackwater marsh.

The first of only two black rail nests ever found in Maryland was located in the Blackwater marsh by Francis Uhler and Arnold Nelson on June 16, 1931. The other was found by Robert E. Stewart and Clark Webster in the Elliott Island marsh, May 20, 1953 (4).

It is of special interest also that the only two winter records of black rails in Maryland are from the Blackwater marsh. The first bird was seen by Claudia Wilds during the southern Dorchester Christmas count, December 26, 1973 (23); the second was observed by Jan Reese on January 16, 1975 (24). These may have been birds that nested locally or in coastal marshes north of Blackwater. Black rails are known to be migratory because specimens have been retrieved at the base of TV towers, lighthouses, and other obstacles that they have struck, particularly along the coast during the spring and fall flight.

Breeding Birds of Blackwater Marshes

The black rail, Virginia rail, clapper rail, king rail, and common gallinule are the five species of Rallidae that nest in the Blackwater marshes. The sora rail is a fairly common migrant, and the very secretive yellow rail, if it occurs, would also be a migrant. The relative abundance of the five local species is not very well known. Rails are more often heard than seen, but judging from the number of calls heard during the nesting season, the Virginia rail would be the most abundant, and the black rail and the common gallinule (Fig. 70) are probably the rarest. The two large rails, the brownish king and grayish clapper, are fairly common. Most of the clappers (Fig. 71) that I have seen were east of the Refuge in saltmarsh cordgrass near Fishing

Fig. 70. The common gallinule, a member of the rail family, is an uncommon nesting bird of the Blackwater area. Ralph Jackson, the Cambridge ornithologist, found a nest with seven eggs near the Blackwater River bridge (highway 335), May 10, 1916. I saw several in the Transquaking River marsh near DeCoursey bridge on June 23, 1976. I have seen them in the fall at Blackwater as late as October 28 (1976), but few if any in winter. Only one has been reported on the southern Dorchester County Christmas count in the last five years. Photograph by Luther Goldman, U.S. Fish and Wildlife Service.

Fig. 71. The clapper rail is mainly a saltmarsh bird, but occasionally occurs in brackish marshes. Its counterpart, the king rail, occurs in fresh and brackish marshes. Where both occur in brackish marshes, they sometimes interbreed. Illustration courtesy of U.S. Fish and Wildlife Service.

Bay, and southwest of the Refuge along the upper Honga River in needlerush habitat (Fig. 72).

The king rail (Figs. 73 and 74) is more evident as it occurs in the fresher marshes which are located near the headquarters area of the Refuge, and often crosses the road (highway no. 335) that leads south along the west side of the Refuge from the Blackwater River bridge through the Gum Swamp section.

Ralph Jackson (1) found a king rail nest of 11 eggs near Sewards, by the Little Blackwater River, on May 19, 1918. A brood of king rail chicks and their parents were seen by P.J. Van Huizen near the Blackwater bridge (highway no. 335) on May 21, 1965. Most of the vegetation in that area is narrowleaf cattail. Approximately 2.2 miles south of the bridge in the Gum Swamp area, I observed an adult king rail and brood on May 8, 1974. The young were approximately ten days old (Fig. 75). Backdating the events from my observations on May 8 to the beginning of nesting, it is apparent that nest building and egg laying began in late March. The incubation period of the king rail is 21-22 days, and clutch size averages 10-11 eggs (Fig. 76). The period of nest building usually lasts from two to six days.

The rail habitat at Gum Swamp is a mixture of shrubs and marsh plants, particularly common rush, a favorite rail nesting plant (Fig. 77). Switchgrass and broadleaf cattail also occur there and are good king rail nest-cover plants. Gum Swamp stands among the best areas for king rails in the Chesapeake Bay Country largely because of its combination of prime habitat with an abundance of crayfish (Fig. 78).

In contrast to the secretive rails is the conspicuous willet with its striking wing pattern (Figs. 79 and 80). Its loud call, *pill-will-willet*, is heard day and night during the courtship period.

Fig. 72. Habitat of the clapper rail and black duck at low tide approximately four miles southwest of Blackwater Refuge along the upper Honga River. Vegetation is mainly needlerush. Periwinkle snails, a food of clapper rails, and ribbed mussels, a minor food of black ducks, were fairly common in this habitat. A brood of young clapper rails was observed here on June 23, 1976. Least bitterns were also seen in the needlerush habitat on that date.

Fig. 73. King rail on a nest constructed of broadleaf cattail plants. Nests are usually placed over water where the depth may range from two or three inches to two feet. In one nest that I found, the eggs were one foot above the normal high-tide level of one foot.

Fig. 74. The author with a king rail caught by placing a long-handled dip net over the nest. The bird was banded and released.

Fig. 75. The author's wife, Anna, banding a king rail chick.

Fig. 76. Nest and 11 eggs of a king rail. The best area that I have found for king rails at Blackwater is in the Gum Swamp section, about two miles south of the Blackwater River bridge on route 335.

Fig. 77. Fresh marsh-shrub swamp habitat of the king rail in the Gum Swamp section along the Church Creek-Hooper Island road (route 335), approximately 2.2 miles south of the Blackwater River bridge. Vegetation is mainly common rush, switchgrass, broadleaf cattail, wax myrtle, and swamp rose. I have seen king rails at this pond on several occasions. Photographed in the spring of 1976.

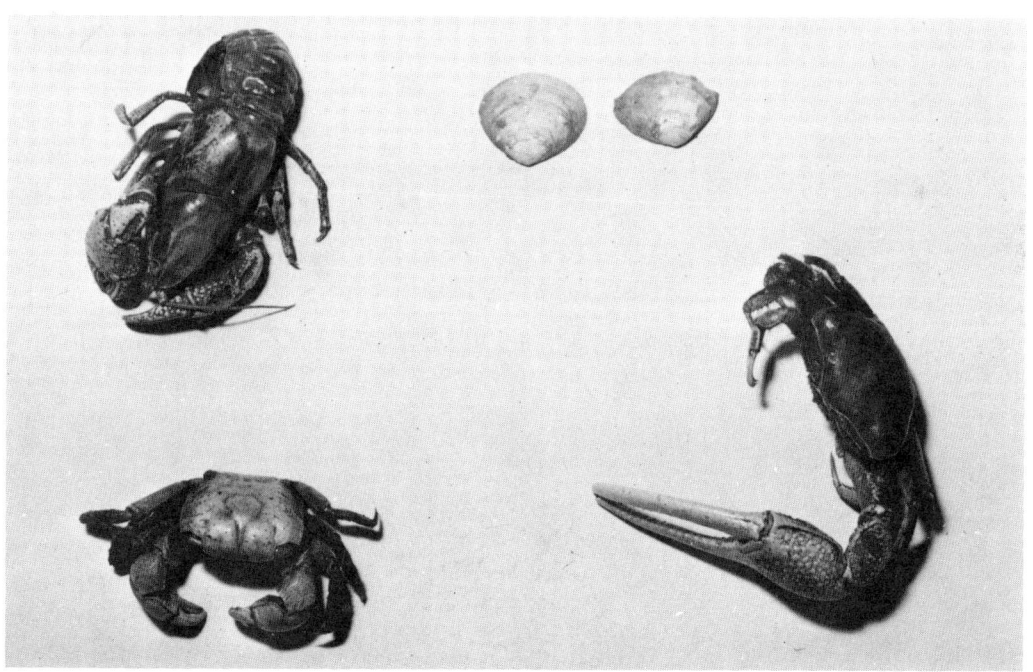

Fig. 78. Some foods of the king rail in Dorchester County marshes. Upper left is crayfish, principal food in fresh marshes; lower left is mud crab; lower right, red-jointed fiddler crab; and upper right, Baltic macoma clams, invertebrate foods found in brackish marshes. Photograph by Matthew C. Perry, U.S. Fish and Wildlife Service.

Fig. 79. Willets characteristically hold their wings aloft for a moment after alighting. The conspicuous wing pattern is important in territory advertisement and defense. The willet's name derives from one of its calls, *pill-will-willet*. The call can be heard day and night during the courtship period. Photograph by Marshall Howe, U.S. Fish and Wildlife Service.

Fig. 80. (Left) Willet hovering over nest. Note striking wing pattern.

Fig. 81. (Right) Nest and eggs of willet.

Breeding Birds of Blackwater Marshes

This large shorebird is a spring and summer resident, arriving at Blackwater in the latter part of April. In the spring of 1976, I saw four pairs on April 23. Most of them nest in the saltmarsh meadow, with clutches laid mostly in mid- and late May (Fig. 81). The earliest nest with eggs that I found was on May 13, 1959.

The height of the nesting season for most birds of the Dorchester County brackish marshes is usually the last week in May and first week in June. On May 28, 1959, I found the following nests with eggs or young: willet, four eggs; red-winged blackbird, four eggs; seaside sparrow, three eggs; sharp-tailed sparrow, four eggs; blue-winged teal, 12 eggs; seaside sparrow, three newly-hatched young; and red-winged blackbird, two newly-hatched young. All were in a saltmeadow cordgrass marsh. Some of these birds renest or have second clutches, a few as late as July.

Fig. 82. Young American bitterns in nest at the Blackwater River marsh. Photograph was made by P. J. Van Huizen in 1935. The least bittern is more common in this area than the American bittern.

At least two nests of the American bittern have been found at Blackwater in July. Such nests appear to be rather uncommon in the area. J.H. Steenis and W.R. Nicholson found one in 1953 (4); and P.J. Van Huizen located a nest in 1935 (Fig. 82).

By the time most species of birds are completing their nesting cycle in the brackish marshes, the short-billed marsh wren is just beginning. In the Blackwater country males seldom establish territories before June. It has been my experience that the short-billed is one of the least abundant nesting songbirds of the Dorchester County brackish estuarine bay marshes. Although Stewart and Robbins (4) list this species as

Fig. 83. Dummy or false nest of a short-billed marsh wren in a mixture of Olney three-square and saltmeadow cordgrass in the Blackwater marsh near Shorter's Wharf, summer 1976. The male short-billed constructs several dummy nests that are like the female's brood nest, except that they are unlined. The brood nest is often lined with wild duck feathers, muskrat or deer hair.

common during the nesting season in tidewater areas of Somerset, Wicomico, and Dorchester Counties, they list only one record of an active nest for the State of Maryland. By contrast, they list 295 nest records for the long-billed marsh wren.

I located two active short-billed marsh wren nests in Dorchester County brackish estuarine bay marshes, both in a mixture of Olney three-square and saltmeadow cordgrass. The first nest was under construction on June 24, 1958, and had six well-incubated eggs on July 12; the second nest had six newly hatched young and one unhatched egg on June 30, 1959, and four surviving nestlings on July 8, which were banded.

On August 16, 1976, I observed a singing male and its mate still on a nesting territory near Shorter's Wharf. The male was the only songbird still singing that I could locate in the marsh that day. It was also singing that night. The song period apparently had ended for the long-billed marsh wren, seaside sparrow, sharp-tailed sparrow, and red-winged blackbird, other songbirds of the brackish marsh. When I worked in the Arkansas rice fields in the early 1950s, I found active short-billed marsh wren nests as late as the second week in September. The wrens did not begin to nest in the rice until mid-July because the plants were not high and dense enough to provide nesting cover prior to that time.

The short-billed and long-billed marsh wrens have similarly constructed nests (Figs. 83 and 84). The short-billed marsh wren's nest is made of finer material and is usually placed from six inches to about a foot above the ground. The long-billed nest

Fig. 84. Female long-billed marsh wren looking out of nest. Rice rats living in the same aquatic environment sometimes take over marsh wren nests.

occurs more in the range of from two to more than five feet. The males of both species build several dummy or false nests. The dummy nests resemble the female's brood nest, except that they do not have the soft interior lining fashioned of wild duck feathers, muskrat hair, and the like.

The short-eared owl may be the rarest nesting bird of the southern Dorchester marshes. Only two nests have been found in Maryland. F.C. Kirkwood, in Stewart and Robbins (4), reported that Orrille Mills found a "marsh owl" nest with eggs in June 1923, and John Warren found a nest of five half-grown young in a brackish marsh near the mouth of the Blackwater River on May 13, 1958. However, so few of the vast Dorchester County marshes have been scouted for nesting birds that the "marsh owl," and some of the other so-called rare nesting birds of the area, may be more common than we suspect.

An idea of the nesting or breeding density of marsh wrens and several other species of birds in brackish estuarine bay marshes is indicated in Table 2.

TABLE 2

*Territorial Male Breeding Bird Population Densities in Brackish Marshes of Dorchester-Somerset Counties, Maryland**

Species	Marsh Type	Terr. Males Per 100 acres	Source
black duck	marsh meadow & other	5.3	Stewart & Robbins (4)
blue-winged teal	saltmarsh meadow	6.2	" " " "
willet	saltmarsh meadow	10.5	" " " "
long-billed marsh wren	needlerush	104.0	Springer & Stewart (25)
short-billed marsh wren	switchgrass & other	10.0	" " " "
red-winged blackbird	saltmarsh meadow	24.0	Meanley & Webb (26)
sharp-tailed sparrow	saltmarsh meadow	100.0	Springer & Stewart (25)
seaside sparrow	saltmarsh meadow	40.0	Meanley — 1977

*Breeding bird population densities listed are for specific areas in brackish marshes, and would vary in other Chesapeake Bay marshes.

Foods of Marsh Ducks

Since most of the Blackwater area is marshland, the majority of the ducks that occur there are dabblers (also known as puddle ducks or shoal-water ducks). They feed in shallow waters and are found in greatest numbers in the winter-half of the year. Among this group mainly are the black duck, mallard, pintail, wigeon (formerly widgeon), gadwall, green-winged and blue-winged teal, and shoveler (Fig. 85). Diving ducks, the canvasback, goldeneye, bufflehead, scaup, redhead, and ruddy, occasionally use small and shallow stillwater ponds as rest and foraging areas, but are associated primarily with larger and deeper bodies of water surrounding the Blackwater marsh—Fishing Bay, Honga River, and the Choptank River. The three mergansers, fish-eating ducks, also occur in the Blackwater area. The hooded merganser is the species primarily associated with the brackish bay marsh community, often frequenting the same ponds as dabbling ducks. The common merganser is usually found in the freshwater impoundments at the Refuge; while the red-breasted occurs in the saltier bodies of water nearby.

In the Blackwater country, dabbling ducks feed mostly in small ponds in the native marsh (Fig. 86); in marshy impoundments on the Refuge; and in the Big and the Little Blackwater Rivers, the Transquaking River, and Meekins Creek. Less frequently they use estuarine brackish bays bordering the marshes.

During the year, many of the small marshy ponds are covered with widgeongrass (Fig. 87) and muskgrass (Fig. 88), an alga, and may also contain other submerged aquatic plants, crustaceans, snails, fish, and aquatic insects, all prime foods of most dabblers.

Most species of marsh ducks generally feed on the same foods, an idea of which may be obtained from a series of 348 stomachs of several species of dabblers collected in brackish estuarine bay marshes, chiefly in southern Dorchester County, as reported by Stewart (3):

"Widgeongrass (leaves, stems, rootstalks, and seeds) is taken in large quantities by nearly all species and is the most important waterfowl food in this habitat. The seeds of Olney three-square represent a major food for many waterfowl species. Other plant foods that are fairly important include: hightide-bush (seeds), saltmarsh bulrush (seeds), and muskgrass. Seeds of twigrush also are frequently taken although this species ordinarily does not grow in brackish estuarine bay marshes. However, twigrush seeds are common in the windrows of vegetative debris along the creeks and ponds of the drainage systems; apparently, these seeds drift down from fresh estuarine bay marshes located on the upper watersheds of many of the tidal streams. Invertebrates commonly eaten by one or more kinds of ducks include the saltmarsh snail *(Melampus bidentatus)*, the tiny gastropod *Littoridinops* sp. [a snail], and copepods [crustaceans]."

Stewart (3) also presented data showing seasonal changes in the food habits of black ducks in southern Dorchester County:

"September, widgeongrass (leaves, stems, and rootstalks) and saltmarsh snails *(Melampus bidentatus)*; October, high-tide bush (seeds), Olney three-square (seeds), widgeongrass (seeds), salt-

Fig. 85. Marsh ducks. Illustrations by Bob Hines, U.S. Fish and Wildlife Service.

Foods of Marsh Ducks

Fig. 86. Brackish marsh habitat of dabbling ducks, especially black duck, mallard, wigeon, gadwall, blue-winged teal, green-winged teal, and shoveler. On May 3, 1977, most of the local breeding ducks of the Blackwater marsh were paired; and on that date there were two pairs of blue-winged teal, a pair of black ducks, and a pair of gadwall feeding in this pond.

marsh bulrush (seeds), and saltmarsh snails; November, widgeongrass (seeds, stems, and rootstalks), Olney three-square (seeds), and twigrush (seeds); December and January, widgeongrass (seeds), leaves, stems, rootstalks, Olney three-square (seeds), fish (chiefly Poecilidae [top minnows or killifishes]); March, saltmarsh snails; and June, mosquitoes (larvae and pupae), saltgrass (leaves, stems, and rootstalks), beetles, and saltmarsh bulrush (seeds)."

Food items found in stomachs are indicators of the environment in which a duck has been feeding. One black duck stomach collected in southern Dorchester County had 18,000 seeds of dotted smartweed in its gullet and stomach. This species of smartweed is associated mainly with fresher marshes. Saltmarsh cordgrass seeds and hulls were the major items in another black duck stomach, indicating that it may have been feeding in a salt marsh. A black duck that had eaten 158 kernels of corn would have been feeding in a corn stubble or taking bait from in front of a duck blind.

Most duck stomachs contain between five and twenty different food items. Sometimes, however, a gullet and/or gizzard may be chock full of a single item. Each of

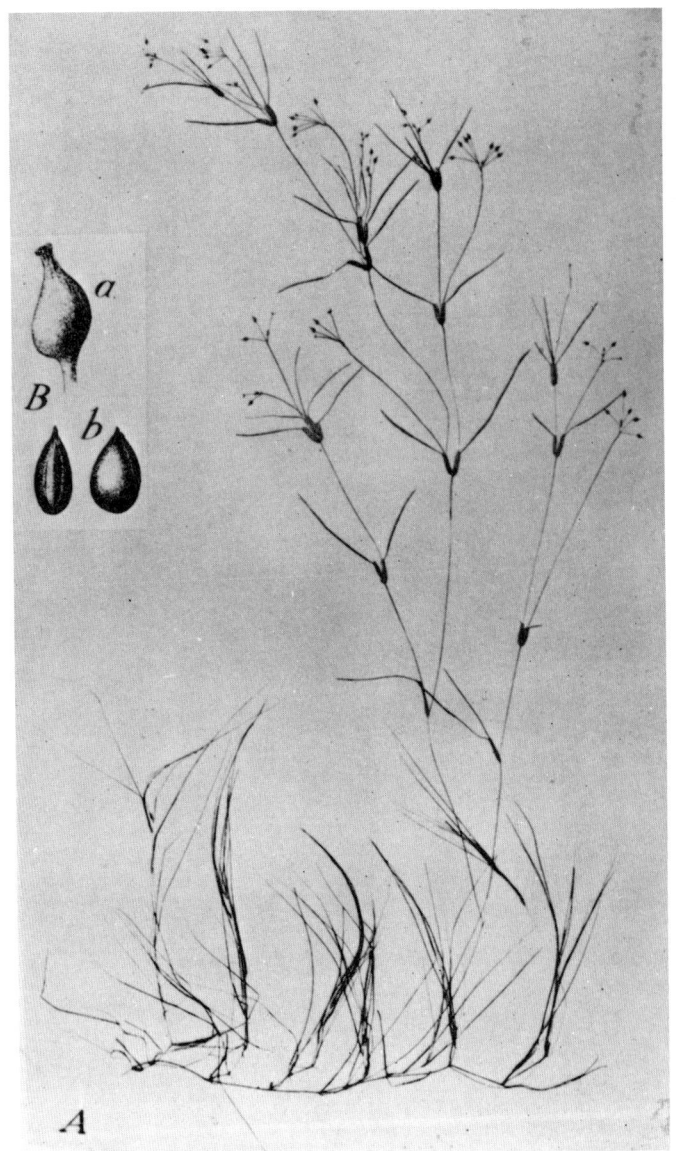

Fig. 87. Widgeongrass. A, specimen. B, seeds (a, normal; b, with outer covering removed).

Widgeongrass, a submerged aquatic, has been one of the most important foods of dabbling ducks and some diving ducks in the Chesapeake Bay area until recently when it became generally scarce. However, it is still locally plentiful in some ponds and tidal guts in the Blackwater marsh. The seeds and vegetative portions are consumed by ducks.

Illustration from *Food of Game Ducks in the United States and Canada*, by A.C. Martin and F.M. Uhler, 1939. Technical Bulletin No. 634, U.S. Dept. of Agriculture, Washington, D.C.

Foods of Marsh Ducks

Fig. 88. Muskgrass from tidal pool in Blackwater brackish marsh. All parts of the plant are consumed by dabbling and diving ducks, but the reproductive structures (oögonia) are especially relished, some 300,000 having been found in a single stomach. Photograph by Matthew C. Perry, U.S. Fish and Wildlife Service.

four wigeon shot by a hunter in Dorchester County brackish marshes had fed on one food item—widgeongrass. Four other wigeon taken in Dorchester marshes had fed only on muskgrass, an alga. The stomach of a wigeon taken in the same general area, was full of another submerged aquatic plant known as eelgrass. Eelgrass is one of the so-called "seaweeds" used by the seafood industry for packing soft crabs, and is an important food of the brant and some of the diving ducks. It grows on tidal flats in two to six feet of water.

The examination of the contents of duck gullets and stomachs for the purpose of identifying food items and determining their frequency and volume is a painstaking microscopic procedure, and often involves the separation of thousands of ground-up particles. Extensive reference collections of aquatic plants, and especially seeds, aquatic insects, mollusks, crustaceans, and fish, are necessary. Francis Uhler, my colleague in the U.S. Fish and Wildlife Service, is the leading authority on this matter, and can identify a plant or animal from the tiniest fragment of a seed coat, snail shell, or insect leg.

I have before me two black duck stomach food analysis cards from our files at the Patuxent Wildlife Research Center that were examined by Mr. Uhler. Both were collected by Robert E. Stewart in southern Dorchester County, on December 31,

1948. One duck had been feeding mostly on plant material and the other on animal matter. The following analyses are fairly representative of the range of foods taken at this season in this locality. Common names of plants and animals are listed, whereas on the cards, scientific names are used (*see* Appendix I for list of scientific names). Plant material comprised 81 percent of the food taken by bird "A" and included:

seeds and hulls of saltmarsh cordgrass	80%
16+ seeds of Olney three-square	1%
2 seeds of twigrush	trace
1 seed of widgeongrass	trace
fragments of a pondweed seed	trace
fragments of dragonfly nymphs	9%
12 snails	4%
fragments of soldier-fly larvae	3%
giant water bug	2%
water scavenger beetle	1%
water boatman	trace
crawling water beetle larva	trace
spider	trace

Animal material comprised 97 percent of the food taken by bird "B" and included:

bones and scales of top minnows	50%
fragments of three giant water bugs	18%
dragonfly nymphs	23%
several dozen small snails (*Littoridina* sp.)	6%
fragments of saltmarsh snails	trace
fragments of a spider	trace
fragments of ostracoda [crustaceans]	trace
62 seeds of twigrush	3%
3 seeds of saltmarsh bulrush	trace
seed fragments of wax myrtle	trace

Odd items sometimes show up in stomachs. A black duck taken in the Blackwater marsh had eaten pine seeds. Pines grow a little way out in the marsh; their seeds drop down into the marsh and can be carried out by the tides. A pintail stomach contained the seeds of blackberry and poison ivy, possibly obtained in a nearby swamp or wooded bottomland.

Stewart lists nearly 100 different food items taken by the several species of marsh ducks in brackish estuarine bay marshes in southern Dorchester County. More detailed information on the food habits of Chesapeake marsh ducks can be found in his *Waterfowl Populations in the Upper Chesapeake Region.*

Birds of Prey of the Marshes

With the exception of studies of food habits of the bald eagle made in the area, there is not much documented evidence of avian predation on mammals and birds of the Blackwater marshes. However, because of the sizable populations of hawks and owls there, and the numerous published reports of predation by these large birds of prey on marsh animals in other localities, there is undoubtedly much predation on meadow voles and other marsh animals by marsh, red-tailed, and red-shouldered hawks, and great horned, short-eared, barn, barred, and screech owls (Figs. 89-91).

Fig. 89. The marsh hawk or harrier (left) and the short-eared owl are the species of hawk and owl most closely associated with eastern marshes. They are the only two birds of prey that nest in Blackwater marshes. Illustrations by Bob Hines, courtesy of the U.S. Fish and Wildlife Service.

No matter how cold or windy the weather or how frozen the substrate, the marsh hawk is the bird that one can invariably see coursing low over the open marsh during any day in winter, hunting for meadow voles and certain other marsh creatures. The short-eared owl is the nocturnal counterpart of the marsh hawk. These two species are the only representatives of their families (hawk and owl) in the Blackwater area that nest and spend most of their time in marshes. Both are much more common in winter than during the nesting season and in summer.

The simplest method of determining the kinds of food that these and other raptors feed on is to examine their regurgitated pellets or castings. When a hawk or owl captures a meadow vole or some other rodent of similar size, it usually consumes the entire animal and later regurgitates the fur and bones as a compact pellet (Fig. 92). The top of a muskrat house is a favorite station for depositing pellets. On two occasions, I have seen a red-tailed hawk drive a marsh hawk from the top of a muskrat house where only seconds earlier it had landed with a meadow vole in its talons. The marsh hawk left the vole on the top of the house as it took off.

Fig. 90. Young barn owls removed from their nest for photographing. Nests are located in hollow trees, duck blinds, and (during the 1940s) in the observation tower at Blackwater Refuge. Bill Julian, manager at Blackwater, told me about a pair of barn owls that nested on the seat of a duck blind in the spring of 1976. A pair of ospreys had a nest on the roof of that blind at the same time. The fact that the osprey is diurnal and the barn owl nocturnal is probably the reason both pairs were successful in fledging young.

Van T. Harris (16) examined 79 pellets from the Blackwater marsh that he believed were those of marsh hawks. An analysis indicated that 73.4 percent of the pellets contained remains of meadow voles, 15.2 percent of rice rats, and 3.8 percent of unidentified small mammals (remaining percentage not reported).

Frank R. Smith (2), also working on the Blackwater marsh, observed that the marsh hawk has the worst reputation of the hawks as a destroyer of muskrats. This is due to its habit of feeding on trapped animals rather than its habit as an independent killer. During Smith's 1933 investigations, five marsh hawks were seen eating trapped muskrats, but at no time during his study was a marsh hawk observed capturing a muskrat.

Birds of Prey of the Marshes

Fig. 91. Screech owls usually feed on mice and insects, and occasionally take birds up to the size of a common grackle. Regurgitated pellets that I found near a screech owl nest at Blackwater mostly contained the remains of meadow mice or voles, known locally as "monks." This is the common mouse of the southern Dorchester County brackish marshes. Illustration by L.A. Fuertes, courtesy of U.S. Fish and Wildlife Service.

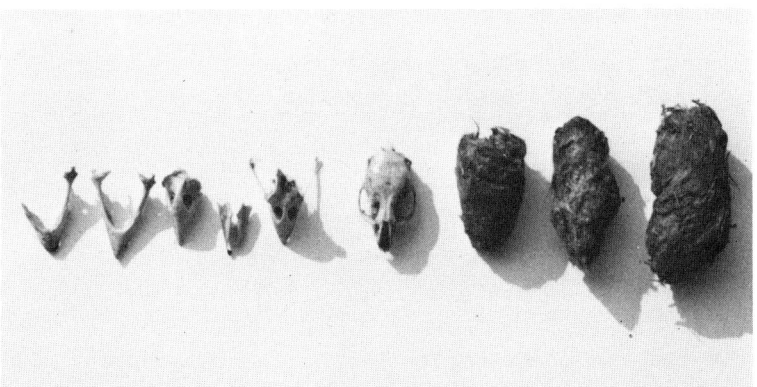

Fig. 92. Three pellets or castings (right side of photograph) of long-eared owl; and skull of mouse and bills or beaks of two cardinals from another one of the owl's pellets.

During the same period, Smith (2) reported on the food remains in a barn owl's nest located in a hollow tree near the Blackwater marsh. The following animals had been eaten: six muskrats, 282 meadow mice or voles, five wood mice, one house mouse, one brown rat, eight short-tailed and six long-tailed shrews, one flying squirrel, one hummingbird, one blackbird, and three unidentified birds.

In nearby Somerset County, D.S. Lee, Arnold Norden, and Barbara Rothgaber (27) collected and examined the contents of 75 pellets regurgitated by barn owls that lived in an old barn close to a marsh. The pellets were collected in March 1971, and contained the following items: 143 meadow voles, 32 rice rats, 19 short-tailed shrews, 14 red-winged blackbirds, one Virginia rail, and six unidentified birds. The investigators stated that the data "strongly imply that these owls do much of their early spring hunting in the neighboring Spartina (saltmarsh grasses) marsh." Meadow voles also live in fields, but since the other items identified were marsh animals, most of the voles were also probably taken there. Red-winged blackbirds roost in marshes, often in large numbers and in compact groups, and would be easy prey for owls.

Otters, Deer, and Raccoons of the Brackish Marshes

Some persons do not generally associate deer, raccoons, and otters with brackish and salt marshes. They usually think of the first two as woodland animals, living only in upland or swampy woods, and the otter as a denizen of streams and rivers. But in the Blackwater country, all three forage in the predominantly brackish marshlands at some time, although their principal retreat may be in the bordering woodlands.

Also, some otters have dens in banks of tidal creeks that wind through the marshes; deer have bedding places in the taller marsh vegetation, such as narrowleaf cattail; and raccoons often take over a deserted or occupied muskrat house for a den of their own.

Otter

For its size, the otter is quite successful at "making itself scarce," for I seldom see one, although I regularly see evidence that some are around a part of the marsh where I am working. However, when I have discovered an active den or some special "hangout," I have been able to observe them frequently over a period of several weeks, and sometimes longer.

Illustration by Bob Hines, U.S. Fish and Wildlife Service.

One April day I observed a pair of otters with two pups, about two-thirds grown, at their den in a ditch bank. I could sit across the ditch ten feet from the den and watch the otter family as long as I wished, as they seemed not to be concerned about me. I could hear the pups occasionally crying and watched them swim two or three feet out into the ditch to meet one of the parents returning after a quarter-mile trip up the ditch and back.

Otters are never far from water, and as pointed out by Lowery (13), "they possess many adaptations for an aquatic existence. The toes are fully webbed, the pelage is water-resistant, and the nostrils and ears can be closed when the animal is submerged. The position of the eyes, near the top of the head, permits the animal to see above the surface while it swims with most of its body beneath the surface of the water."

An otter that I saw regularly along a ditch one spring appeared to do most of its feeding in the evening beginning at about 5:00 p.m. Since there was a trail beside the ditch, it was possible to follow the otter as it swam mostly underwater searching for food. Once I followed the otter for nearly three-fourths of a mile as it swam along under the water. I could stay parallel with it because I could always determine where it was by a string of bubbles trailing behind. Each time it caught something it would surface, and with head and neck out of water and nose pointed nearly straight up, it would chew its food for a few seconds, and then dive to resume swimming and fishing underwater. Otters feed mostly on fish, crayfish, crabs, frogs, and aquatic insects.

In the Blackwater country most of the otter signs that I see are in the saltmarsh meadows near tidal guts (creeks). The grass in saltmeadows is seldom over a foot in height and is often windblown. Otter trails lead across the meadow from one tidal gut to another or from a gut to a stillwater pond. Otters are known to be playful, and must do a lot of rolling around along their trails as the grass is often matted down for a width of several feet on both sides. These marsh trails are usually strewn with scales of fish and fragments of crustaceans where they have been feeding or made their toilets.

Deer

There are a number of pine woods islands in the southern Dorchester marshes. Deer trails lead from one island to another. Rails, raccoons, muskrats, and other marsh creatures use these deer trails in moving about the marsh, and so do I. Most of the pine islands have an understory of deciduous shrubs and vines, some of which are important foods of deer. Some marsh plants also are eaten, especially sedges; and in the fresher ponds I have seen them feeding on the leaves and stems of water lilies.

Blackwater deer also forage in the pine woods and mixed pine-hardwoods along the mainland bordering the extensive brackish marshes, and in corn and soybeans at the Refuge, grown especially for Canada geese.

Illustration by Bob Hines, USFWS.

Deer are essentially browsers, their native diet consisting chiefly of tender shoots, leaves, and twigs, acorns, and fruits. The following plants have a high palatability rating with Blackwater deer: smilax or greenbrier, oak (especially acorns), dogwood, and Japanese honeysuckle. Less important but also utilized are red maple, black gum, and sassafras.

The abundance of native plant foods, supplemented by cultivated crops, should continue to sustain the herd of an estimated 300 deer at the 11,000-acre Blackwater Refuge.

Raccoon

I believe that most studies of raccoons at Blackwater Refuge have been concerned with predation on muskrats and black duck eggs. Such investigations have also revealed some interesting facts concerning the varied diet of this carnivore or "omnivore."

Illustration by Bob Hines, USFWS.

Van T. Harris (16) examined 551 raccoon droppings at Blackwater during the period 1949-1951. Approximately 20 percent of the droppings had evidence of muskrats. However, it is not known to what extent raccoon predation truly affects muskrat populations in the Blackwater area. As Van Harris points out, to determine this, it would be necessary to know the size of the muskrat and raccoon population on the Blackwater marsh.

It is of interest to note that when raccoons seek out a muskrat house they are not always bent on destruction. In one Delaware marsh, biologists found a raccoon and a family of muskrats sharing the same house with neither one disturbing the other (28).

Food items taken by Blackwater raccoons, as indicated by the Van Harris study, were, in order of importance, fish, mice, vegetation and fruit, crabs, muskrats, birds, and corn.

In a brackish marsh along Delaware Bay, I frequently observed a raccoon digging small clams *(Macoma balthica)* in the bed of a tidal creek at low tide. A king rail with a brood of half-grown young also fed on clams at the same spot.

Raccoon predation on black duck nests appears to be minimal. Vern Stotts of the Maryland Game and Inland Fish Commission and David E. Davis of Johns Hopkins University (21) found in their study of the breeding behavior and biology of the black duck in the Chesapeake area that, while 50 percent of all clutches of eggs in this study were destroyed, raccoons were responsible for only about six percent. Crows destroyed about 70 percent of the eggs. Most of the clutches destroyed by raccoons were located in duck blinds near shore.

The Swamp Owl

Marshlands and pine woods are the principal plant communities in the Blackwater country, with small patches of upland hardwoods and several fairly extensive hardwood and mixed pine-hardwood swamps as secondary areas. Because the land is low almost everywhere in the Blackwater region, some loblolly pine woods that extend out toward the marshes can be called pine swamps, as the ground in the stands is frequently flooded for long periods of time.

But the hardwood swamp is the domain of the barred owl (Fig. 93), sometimes referred to in Blackwater country as the swamp owl. Barred owls also hunt over the marshlands and occasionally in the pinelands, but the base of operations is almost always the hardwood swamp.

Fig. 93. The barred or swamp owl is one of seven species of owls that occur at Blackwater. It is mainly associated with lowland hardwoods and pine-hardwoods plant communities. Photograph by Frederick C. Schmid, U.S. Fish and Wildlife Service.

The Swamp Owl

The barred owl's counterpart in the pine woods is the great horned owl. I believe that one of the reasons the barred owl is more a bird of the hardwoods than pine woods is because in this locality it usually nests in large cavities (Figs. 94-96), and pine trees seldom have such large hollow nesting sites. Also, since the pine woods is the principal range of the great horned owl, which is slightly larger and is dominant, the barred owl is generally excluded.

An interesting ecological relationship exists between the barred owl and the red-shouldered hawk of the hardwood swamps and the great horned owl and red-tailed hawk of the pine woods. In their respective habitats, both species of owls are the nocturnal equivalent of the two hawks. Arthur C. Bent has remarked on this relationship between the barred owl and red-shouldered hawk in his *Life Histories of North American Birds of Prey* (29): "I have always considered these two as complementary and friendly species; their haunts and their food are very similar; one

Fig. 94. Barred owl flies from hollow tree nest.

Fig. 95. Nest and eggs of barred owl, March 20, 1937.

The Swamp Owl

Fig. 96. Young barred owls in this hollow tree nest had been fed a crayfish, a flicker, and a woodcock, as evidenced by food remains in the nest on April 25, 1936.

hunts exclusively by day and the other largely by night or twilight in the same locality. They often use the same nests alternately and rarely even simultaneously; almost always there is a red-shouldered hawk's nest in the same patch of woods with the barred owl; once I found the occupied hawk's nest within 24 yards of the owl's nest." Mr. Bent was writing about barred owls in white pine woods near his home in Massachusetts where these raptors often nest in the old hawk, crow, or squirrel nests, as well as hollow trees. Of the 30 or so barred owl nests that I have seen in Maryland, all were in hollow limbs or stumps, or some sort of cavity, rather than in open abandoned nests of hawks (Fig. 97) or crows.

In his narrative on this owl, Mr. Bent incorporates the notes of another ornithologist who found two red-shouldered hawk nests containing eggs of both the hawk and the barred owl.

Fig. 97. Nest and eggs of red-shouldered hawk. Barred owls sometimes lay eggs in deserted hawk or crow nests. The red-shouldered hawk, also a bird of the hardwood swamps, is the diurnal counterpart of the barred owl.

Fig. 98. Newly-hatched barred owls. Note that egg tooth on tip of bill is still present. The egg tooth, used to cut the shell from the inside when the chick is ready to free itself from the egg, will fall off in a few days. Birds in this picture were removed from nest for photographing.

One nest contained three eggs of the hawk and one of the owl, and the owl was incubating; the other had two eggs of the hawk and one of the owl, and the hawk was incubating.

The usual clutch of the barred owl is two to three eggs. In Dorchester County, Ralph Jackson (1) reported seven nests with the average laying date of eggs as March 23rd. I found a nest with nestlings as early as March 23 (1935). The eggs must have been laid in February (Fig. 98).

Six nests that I found had remains of food fed to young. Crayfish and flickers were found at three nests, and a woodcock, blue jay, starling, mole, and fish at others.

On February 10, 1977, I saw a barred owl perched on a limb about 30 feet from a Delmarva fox squirrel that was on the ground feeding on a kernel of corn. As I moved slightly, the owl was frightened and flew off. I wonder if it had designs on the squirrel? A.C. Bent (29) reports that fox squirrels have been taken by barred owls. P.T. Blogg (30) saw a red-tailed hawk struggling with a Delmarva fox squirrel in Dorchester County. A barred owl is about the same size as a red-tailed hawk, but the owl usually tackles prey smaller than fox squirrels.

Judging from the one or two barred owls reported on the annual Christmas bird count in southern Dorchester County, this raptor would appear to be uncommon in that area. However, some of the best areas for barred owls at Blackwater are in Gum and Moneystump Swamps, and both are just outside of the 15-mile Christmas count circle.

Spring and Fall Migration of Birds at Blackwater

Although most birds migrate in the spring and fall, their seasonal movements might more aptly be termed northward and southward migration, since individuals of one species or another are migrating during every month of the year. The Blackwater area, being in the middle latitudes and near the coast, experiences this phenomenon more than most regions. In Maryland, the Chesapeake Bay Country is second only to the Atlantic Coast as a major flyway of migratory birds; and as Blackwater is part of this system it is an important concentration area for birds moving north and south. The 11,000-acre Refuge and surrounding territory with its vast marshlands, waterways, and pine woodlands provide a resting place and an abundance of food along the main corridor of travel.

In mild winters by early February, the first Canada geese (Fig. 99), red-winged blackbirds (Fig. 100), and whistling swans are migrating through or leaving the Chesapeake Bay Country, although the peak flight northward for these species is not under way until a month or six weeks later. In the second half of February and the first part of March, some species that do not winter very far south—the woodcock, killdeer, robin, bluebird, phoebe, and American bittern—are arriving in small numbers.

When I visited Blackwater on March 24, 1976, I noted 650 common snipe, 30 greater yellowlegs, and 20 dunlins feeding in the mud flats at low tide; a pair of ospreys that had returned from winter quarters in South America were already building a nest; and a noticeable increase in the pine warbler population (a few pine warblers, dunlins, snipe, and yellowlegs usually winter in southern Dorchester County and occur there during every month of the year, but only the warblers nest there).

By the last week in March, tree swallows and purple martins have returned; there is a marked increase in the number of migrating shovelers and ring-billed gulls (some of both winter in the area); and blue-gray gnatcatchers and Louisiana waterthrushes, first of the songbirds from the tropics, arrive at Blackwater.

By mid-April, laughing gulls are following the plows and harrows, replacing ring-bills, most of which have moved onward toward the Great Lakes; and the majority of the migrant marsh birds have returned. On April 19, 1977, I noted the following: 45 snowy egrets, 30 great egrets, 15 cattle egrets, 16 willets (already paired), two glossy ibis, and one seaside sparrow. Also on that date, migrants that had stopped off to feed in the shallow tidal pools before proceeding northward included an estimated 2,000 greater yellowlegs, 150 lesser yellowlegs, 500 dunlins, and 70 green-winged teal. Blue-winged and green-winged teal, the earliest of the fall migrant waterfowl to arrive at Blackwater, are the latest to pass through in the spring.

Fig. 99. Canada geese strung out over the Transquaking River near Blackwater Refuge in February, shortly before the beginning of their flight northward toward the Hudson Bay-Ungava Peninsula nesting grounds.

Fig. 100. Red-winged blackbirds "on the move." Redwings are usually the first spring or northward migrants from the South to arrive at Blackwater. Some remain to establish nesting territories; others pass through. Photograph courtesy of the U.S. Fish and Wildlife Service.

In the Blackwater area, the northward migration of songbirds peaks in late April and early May. Most of our local nesting songbird population arrives with this massive flight. On April 25, 1976, orchard orioles, prairie warblers, ovenbirds, wood thrushes, crested flycatchers, and house wrens had returned to the mixed pine-hardwoods habitat.

Northward migration tapers off in June, with a few late migrating warblers, thrushes, and shorebirds still passing through. On June 20, 1976 at Blackwater, Henry Armistead (31) noted four semipalmated plovers, four semipalmated sandpipers, and a white-rumped sandpiper. At this late date, one wonders whether these shorebirds were passing through or were nonbreeding birds, possibly immatures, that had halted their migration at this point.

Although July may seem like the "dead of summer" for bird activity, actually southward migration is well under way during that period. This is often quite evident along the river marshes where at that time swallows and kingbirds follow the south-trending streams, attracted by the hordes of insects; and ruby-throated hummingbirds are lured by jewelweed and other flowering plants of the summer marsh. On reaching the Gulf Coast, the tiny hummingbird makes the 500-mile journey across the Gulf of Mexico and returns by the same general route in the spring.

By late July and early August, the northern waterthrush, perhaps the earliest southward migrant of the warbler family, and a bird that lives in a northern swampy environment in the spring, may be encountered in southward migration at Blackwater in a wet pine woods, a marsh, or even a cornfield.

Blue-winged teal and sora or Carolina rails from breeding grounds north of Chesapeake Bay, are arriving at Blackwater on their southward migration in the first half of August. The northern blue-winged teal population augments the local Blackwater teal population, and by mid-fall most of them have passed on to the tropics. Blue-winged teal banded at Blackwater in early fall have been recovered in Cuba, Bahama Islands, Dominican Republic, Puerto Rico, Barbados, Trinidad, British Guiana, and Brazil (4).

The green-winged teal, our smallest duck, arrives at Blackwater from breeding grounds in Labrador, Newfoundland, and the Maritime Province shortly after the first bluewings, or in late August. Most greenwings in this flyway winter from the Chesapeake Bay Country through tidewater Virginia and the Carolinas.

The larger ducks, mallard, pintail, shoveler, and some of the others, begin to arrive in the Blackwater area in September, with the main flight in October and November. On September 22, 1976, I saw an estimated 2,000 mallards, 500 pintails, six wigeon, and an early small contingent of Canada geese at Blackwater Refuge. By October 28, there were an estimated 80,000 Canada geese and 1,200 snow geese at the Refuge.

At the same time that many kinds of birds are arriving from the north, there are still some holdovers from the summer that will soon be moving south. Among the last of these departures are those of the herons and egrets. On September 22, 1976 at Blackwater, I counted 70 cattle egrets, 23 great egrets (Fig. 101), 14 snowy egrets, three little blue herons, and two Louisiana herons.

The songbird migration peaks in late September and early October. One of the last of the so-called songbirds to pass through is the tree swallow. On October 28, 1976, I observed 3,000 tree swallows near Shorter's Wharf, along the Blackwater River. The temperature was in the low 40 degrees F. that afternoon. Insects were in

Fig. 101. Great egrets (formerly known as American or common egrets) are common summer residents that feed in Blackwater marshes. They arrive from the South in April and usually depart by late September. I counted 23 still at Blackwater on September 22, 1976. Photograph by Luther Goldman, U.S. Fish and Wildlife Service.

short supply, and the tree swallows were feeding on wax myrtle berries, a well-known alternative food of these hardy birds (Fig. 102). This abundant food is vitally important to the few that may remain through the winter.

During the two hours that I watched the swallows, they fed as a flock, descending together on the myrtle bushes every 15 to 20 minutes. When I visited the area on November 3, only 20 tree swallows were observed. It was much warmer and the swallows were coursing the marshes for insects.

Fig. 102. Wax myrtle berries, important fall and winter food of tree swallows in the Blackwater marsh area when temperatures are low and mosquitoes and other flying insects are not available.

The earliest songbird migrants in the spring, the blackbirds, are among the latest in the fall. The red-winged blackbird, common grackle, and brown-headed cowbird, all members of the blackbird family, the Icteridae, reach the peak of their fall migration at Blackwater in October and November. They migrate later than most birds because their postnuptial or postjuvenal molt is not completed until about October 1, and because most of them spend the winter only as far south as the Carolinas. Most species of birds do not undertake a sustained southward migration until the molt is complete, or virtually so.

I have been especially impressed with the fall movement of common grackles because their foraging habits in the hardwood forests at that time of the year are much like those of the now-extinct passenger pigeons of a century ago. Great flocks of grackles, sometimes numbering five to ten thousand, filter through the hardwoods from the tops of the trees to the leaf mantle of the forest floor, searching for an assortment of plant and animal foods (Fig. 103).

As was the case with the passenger pigeon, acorn and beech mast are staple foods for the grackle, but they are supplemented with fruits of native shrubs, trees, and vines, including black gum, dogwood, poison ivy, and dried grapes. Constantly on the move, the great flocks of grackles scour the woodland floor overturning leaves

Spring and Fall Migration of Birds at Blackwater 103

Fig. 103. In the fall, usually in October, flocks of migrating common grackles drift through the hardwood forests from the tops of the trees to the leaf mantle of the forest floor, searching for an assortment of plant and animal foods. Constantly on the move, the great flocks scour the woodland floor, overturning leaves and sticks in search of hibernating insects, worms, snails, and frogs. From time to time they move out into the open country to feed in corn stubble fields. Photograph by F.C. Schmid, U.S. Fish and Wildlife Service.

and sticks in search of hibernating insects, worms, snails, and frogs. On one occasion I observed grackles feeding in a beechnut tree, and as they crushed the nuts, fragments fell to the ground where they were eaten by a dozen or so waiting robins.

Because of the small size, acorns eaten by grackles are usually those of pin and willow oaks. These are the same ones known to have been taken by the passenger pigeons (32).

Most of the October grackles are purple-backed birds indicating they come mostly from the Middle Atlantic States, perhaps from as far north as New York. Some of the November birds are bronzed-backed, from farther north, New England and eastern Canada.

By about Thanksgiving, most common grackles (both the purple and bronzed types) destined for wintering grounds in eastern Virginia and the Carolinas, have passed through, and those remaining in Dorchester and Somerset Counties have formed large roosts, several of which number over a million birds.

The last of the common grackles, red-winged blackbirds, robins, and waterfowl migrating southward through the Blackwater country in December, may some miles farther south meet the first red-winged blackbirds migrating northward in January!

The Christmas Bird Count in Southern Dorchester County

One day during each Christmas season, usually between December 18 and January 2, a census of the birdlife of southern Dorchester County, Maryland, is conducted by a group of ornithologists for the purpose of keeping track of changing bird populations in that area. The southern Dorchester count, started in 1947, and now in its 30th year, is one of approximately 20 Christmas bird counts made each year in Maryland, and over 1,000 made nationwide (1,141 in 1975).

Fig. 104. Veteran birders Luther Goldman (foreground) and John Taylor have participated in southern Dorchester and other Maryland Christmas counts.

The Christmas Bird Count, sponsored by the National Audubon Society, was inspired by Frank M. Chapman, Curator of Birds at the American Museum of Natural History in New York. There were 27 participants on 25 counts that first year in 1900, and 28,688 in the 1975 counts, which have become the greatest cooperative ornithological project in North America.

The procedures for Christmas counts are the same nationwide. The count area, usually the same in each geographical region, is a circle 15 miles in diameter. The southern Dorchester County area of interest is mainly in the Blackwater and Elliott

Island areas, with the center of the circle located approximately five miles north of Wingate. Habitat coverage is estimated as: brackish marsh, 33 percent; loblolly pine woods 20 percent; hedgerows and edge, 17 percent; open fields, 11 percent; ponds, bays, and estuaries, 7 percent; swamps, 7 percent; and upland deciduous woods, 5 percent.

In most recent years, the number of participants in the southern Dorchester counts ranged between 15 and 35 persons. Chandler S. Robbins, prominent ornithologist, is the leader and compiler. He assigns specific areas to teams of birders who gather the night before or at a predawn breakfast for their assignments and any other instructions that are necessary (Fig. 104). Most participants get very little sleep the night before the count, and some even stay up in order to be ready to go out and listen for owls beginning one minute after midnight. At the end of the day, the group assembles at a predetermined location to tally the results of the day in the field. The 132 species observed on the 1975 count (December 31), was the highest in 30 years. A list of species, showing the number of years observed and the highest and lowest numbers for each, is presented in Appendix I.

Note: Data presented in this account are from *Audubon Field Notes* and *American Birds*, publications of the National Audubon Society.

The number of species varies little from year to year compared to the variation in number of individuals seen. The wide variation in numbers is usually caused by someone seeing a huge flock of blackbirds (common grackles or red-winged blackbirds) or some waterfowl species one year and relatively few in a subsequent year. For example, in 1961, some 500,000 red-winged blackbirds were reported, whereas in 1975 there were only 3,170.

Since one of the objectives of the Christmas Bird Count is to note trends in bird populations, a good example is demonstrated by the increase in Canada geese and snow geese in the years of the southern Dorchester count. In 1947, the first year of the count, 1,570 Canada geese were reported; in 1952, 15,000, and in 1962, 46,625. In the last five years there have been between 30,000 and 45,000. In 1948, only one snow goose was listed, whereas by 1965, there were 955, and in 1976, 3,014 (Fig. 105). By contrast, there has been a decline in the number of brown-headed nuthatches in the last ten years (Fig. 106).

The highlight of the Christmas Bird Count is sighting a rare or unusual bird, viz., one that should be in the tropics at that time of the year, one of the warblers or thrushes; or one from the far north, perhaps a snowy owl; or a local species like a red-cockaded woodpecker, that is rare at any time. Then there are those birds that are known to be fairly common in the area, but are difficult to find, like the rails. Seeing some of these birds often presents a real challenge (they are usually *heard*).

Actually, there are many highlights on a Christmas bird count. For southern Dorchester County, I would list the following:

Bald and golden eagles. Bald eagles are on the rare and endangered species list. Blackwater is a known bald eagle concentration area and they are expected to be

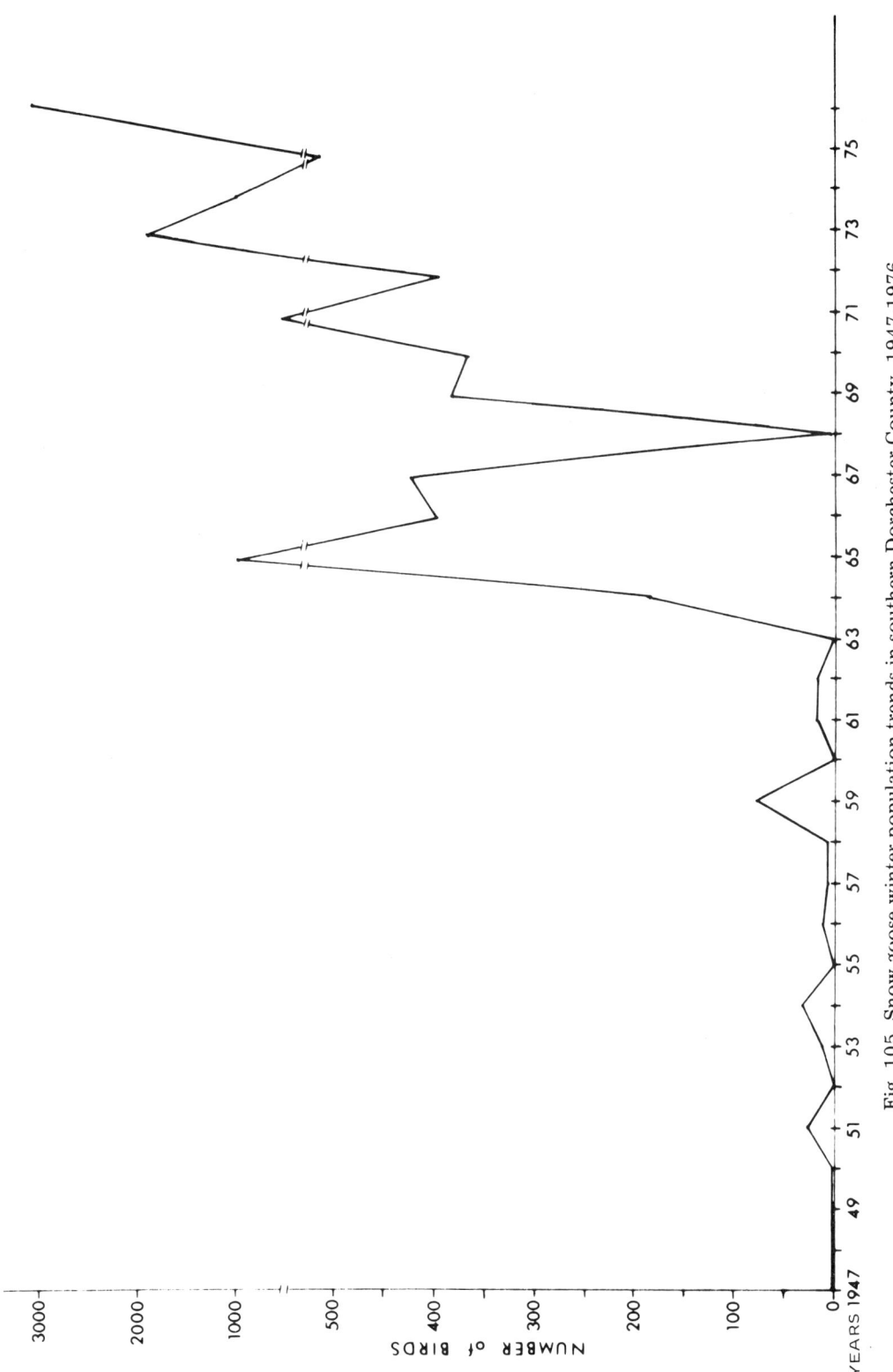

Fig. 105. Snow goose winter population trends in southern Dorchester County, 1947-1976.

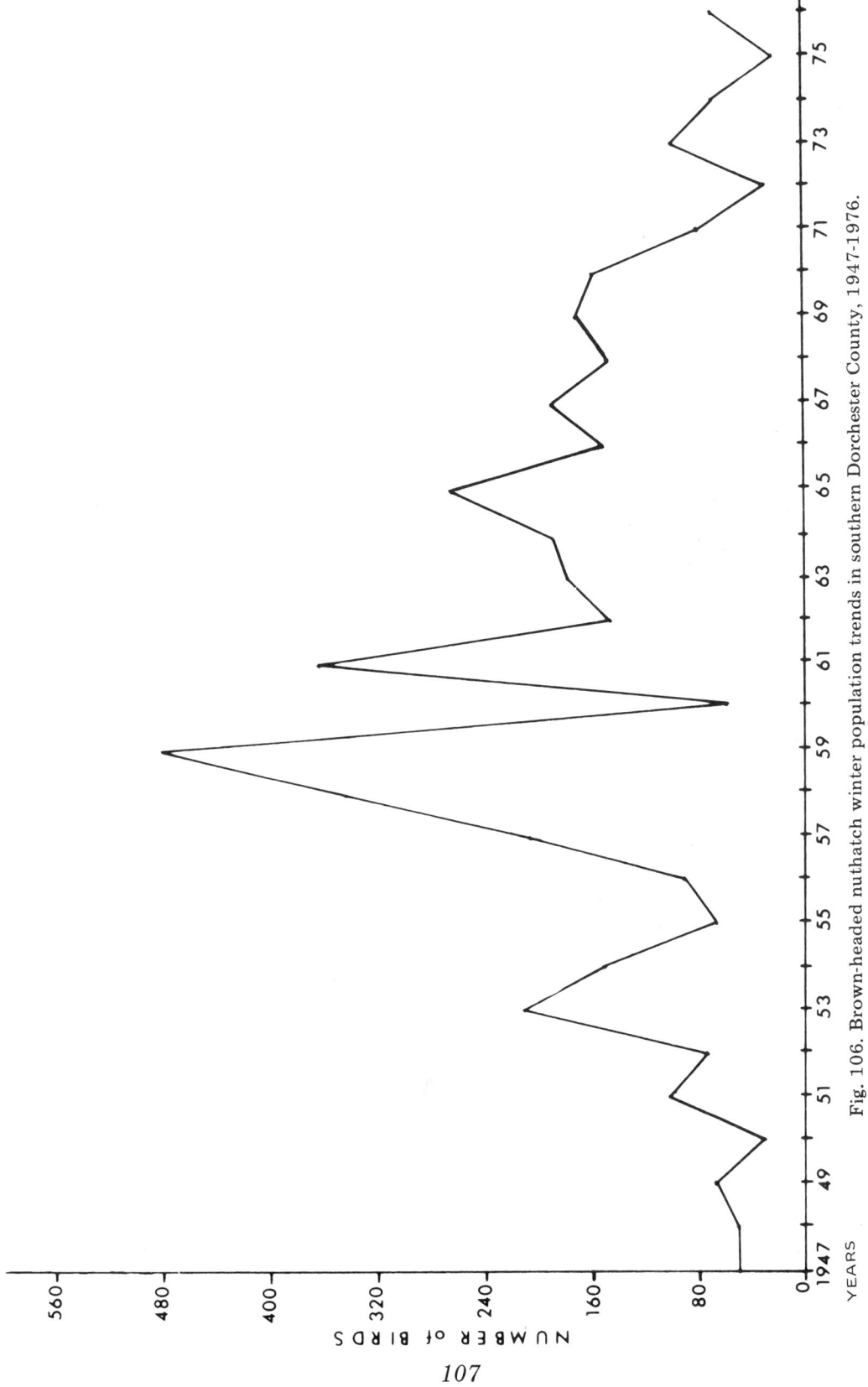

Fig. 106. Brown-headed nuthatch winter population trends in southern Dorchester County, 1947-1976.

seen, especially at the Refuge. Yet their numbers are impressive in most winters and this is significant. On the December 26, 1975 count, 25 were seen; the year before, 35. One to three golden eagles are usually present. Golden eagles drift in from the far west or far north, and are always a rare sight.

Northern finches. Some members of the finch family from the North are regular winter visitors, such as the purple finch and pine siskin. Some are sporadic, like the red crossbill (223 in 1975) and evening grosbeak (400 in 1975), and their occurrence in the Middle Atlantic States can sometimes be predicted because the seeds of coniferous and other trees upon which they feed in the North are in short supply. Other northern finches would be rare at any time, and would include the white-winged crossbill (1 in 1969), pine grosbeak (2 in 1968), and common redpoll (2 in 1968).

Other northern birds. A few rough-legged hawks (usually about 10, but 27 in 1944) are observed each winter. One of the field characters that is a clue to their identification is their habit of hovering over a marsh or open field like the smaller sparrow hawk or kestrel. A northern hawk rarely seen is the goshawk; only one has been reported on the 30 years of The Southern Dorchester County Christmas Bird Count. Red-breasted nuthatches are sporadic winter visitors whose southern incursions can be spurred by severe winters and food shortages in the North. Thirty-four were seen in 1975.

Warblers. The warblers are members of one of our largest families of birds. Some 37 species occur in Maryland, either as breeding birds or transients. Usually only three or four species are reported on southern Dorchester Christmas counts. The yellow-rumped warbler is consistently and usually abundantly present (Fig. 107). A few (usually less than 10) pine warblers and common yellowthroats, and one or two palm warblers, are reported nearly every winter. Most of the other species are in Central or South America by Christmastime. Thus any other warbler that turns up at this season is a big surprise. A Nashville warbler spotted on the 1974 count, was the third Maryland winter record for that species. Orange-crowned warblers, breeding birds of the far western states, winter in the southwestern and southeastern United States, but seldom as far north as Maryland. One seen on the December 31, 1957 count was the first for the southern Dorchester Christmas count.

Shorebirds. Before I became involved in Christmas counts in the 1940s, I assumed that sandpipers, yellowlegs, and snipe wintered only in the southern latitudes. But we are finding out that they winter in considerable numbers in Delmarva. High numbers for snipe were 93 in 1974, and for dunlins, 444 in 1975. Usually under 20 greater yellowlegs are seen on each count, and fewer lesser yellowlegs.

Robins, bluebirds, gray catbirds, and brown thrashers. These four species that we see around our homes in spring and summer, and that have departed by fall, regularly show up on Christmas counts. The climate is a little milder in the lower Bay area and this is actually about the northern limit of the winter range of these species.

Fig. 107. Most of the myrtle or yellow-rumped warblers in the East follow the coastal bayberry or wax myrtle belt in the fall and winter and are abundant in southern Dorchester County where this plant grows. As many as 6,500 have been recorded on a one-day Christmas count in the Blackwater-Elliott Island area. Illustration by L.A. Fuertes, courtesy of U.S. Fish and Wildlife Service.

The robin is more of a woodland bird at this season, in contrast to its summer front-lawn habitat. A total of 2,570 was listed in 1973, and 1,210 in 1974. There were 147 bluebirds in 1957, and 133 in 1958. Catbirds and brown thrashers usually total under 20 birds each on the Christmas count.

Owls. Owls are definitely a specialty item or some bird counters would not stay up all night to add them to their lists. The seven species reported on the 1974 count included the barn owl (4), screech owl (24), great horned owl (32), barred owl (2), long-eared owl (13), short-eared owl (13), and saw-whet owl (2). That same winter, a snowy owl, summer resident of the arctic region, was observed for several days at Cambridge, about 10 miles north of the Refuge. As for the long-eared owls, although the official count published for that species was 13, it was determined later that there were fewer. Apparently someone not familiar with the call of a nutria, an introduced marsh mammal from South America, heard several calling at night and mistook them for long-eared owls.

Fig. 108. The Cooper's hawk is an uncommon winter resident, and seldom more than two are reported on the southern Dorchester Christmas count. Hooper Island is a concentration point for these migrating hawks in the fall. Several birds recovered in Dorchester County had been banded in Massachusetts. Illustration by Louis A. Fuertes, courtesy of U.S. Fish and Wildlife Service.

Rails. Six species of Rallidae have been reported from southern Dorchester County on winter counts. The Virginia rail is the most common, with 115 reported in 1974. Kings and clappers are regularly reported, the sora occasionally, and the black rail and common gallinule (also a rail), rarely. The tiny black rail, no larger than a sparrow, is the most secretive of this shy family of birds, and only one (1973) has been noted on the southern Dorchester count. The second of only two known wintering black rails in Maryland was seen and heard by Jan Reese after the count period, on January 16, 1975. Both birds were seen at Blackwater National Wildlife Refuge.

Cooper's hawk (Fig. 108). This species is declining in numbers in this area and probably throughout its range. In 1947, nine observers on the southern Dorchester count saw seven; but from 1970 to 1975, no more than two were seen each year by two or three times the number of observers as in 1947. Henny (33) estimated a 25 percent annual rate of decline for the population in the northeastern United States during the period 1949-67. Hackman and Henny (34) reported a 13 percent annual rate of decline in the fall migration at White Marsh, Maryland, between the years 1951 and 1961. The problem is due to low reproductive success, apparently due to pollutants, which cause eggshell thinning.

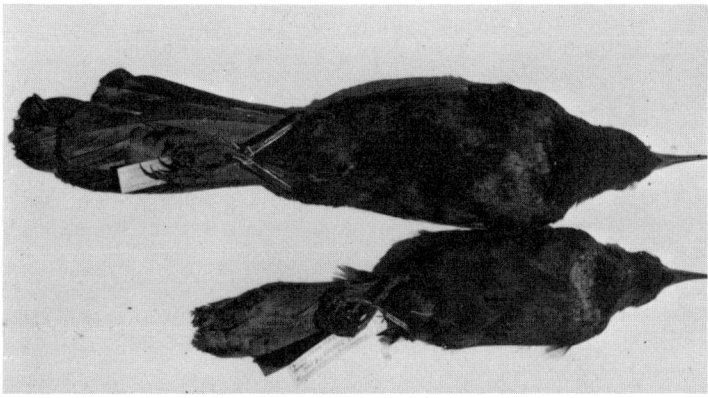

Fig. 109. Museum study skins of a male boat-tailed grackle (top) and a common grackle. The larger boat-tail is mostly a marine species, feeding about marshes, and is uncommon in the Blackwater area. The common grackle, an upland species, is usually abundant on Christmas counts in southern Dorchester County, where 150,000 were reported on December 31, 1958.

Some high counts of less well-known birds are 164 short-billed marsh wrens in 1951; 482 brown-headed nuthatches in 1959; and 475 boat-tailed grackles (Figs. 109 and 110) in 1969. Although a possibly better known species, I think that the total of 1,255 tree swallows counted in 1957 is notable. Since we usually associate swallows with summertime, for me it was indeed a strange sight to see tree swallows flying about in a snowstorm on an Eastern Shore Christmas count. While other species of swallows are mainly down in the tropics at this season, the hardy tree swallow survives in cold weather by feeding on the berries of wax myrtle, a shrub of the maritime pine forests and marsh edges.

Among some rarities seen only once on the southern Dorchester counts are the Bachman's sparrow, a southern bird well north of its range (December 31, 1957); red-cockaded woodpecker, at the northern limit of its range (December 31, 1958); Lapland longspur, a bird from the north and usually much farther west of Maryland at this season (December 29, 1969); Swainson's thrush, a bird that should be in the tropics at Christmastime (December 31, 1957); and a gannet, an oceanic species that was probably blown inland during a storm (December 31, 1958).

I wonder what's going to turn up next year?

Fig. 110. Boat-tailed grackles hunting over a needlerush-saltgrass marsh approximately five miles south of the Blackwater River. In that area they feed mostly on fiddler crabs, aquatic insects, and seeds of aquatic plants. Boat-tails reach their northern limit along the Chesapeake in the Fishing Bay-Hooper Island areas. Their range along the Atlantic Coast extends from Florida to New Jersey.

The Whistling Swan on the Wintering Ground

The Chesapeake Bay winters more whistling swans than any other area (Fig. 111). Of an estimated 123,000 whistlers in the continental population, approximately 40,000 winter in the Chesapeake Bay Country. Some 14,000 winter in areas extending from Back Bay, Virginia (near Norfolk), through Lake Mattamuskeet and Pamlico Sound in eastern North Carolina. Most of the other whistling swans winter in the Pacific Flyway, with largest concentrations in the San Francisco Bay area (6).

Fig. 111. One whistling swan is asleep, the other is watching the photographer. Icy edge of the Choptank River about 10 miles north of Blackwater. Photograph by John W. Taylor.

In the fall, whistling swans destined for Chesapeake Bay wintering grounds migrate south from the northwest arctic and subarctic tundra breeding areas, by way of northern Alberta and Saskatchewan, Devils Lake area of North Dakota, across the Great Lakes to the Middle Atlantic area (Fig. 112). Some come from as far as the Alaskan Northern Slope near the Prudhoe Bay oil fields.

During fall migration, according to Bellrose (6), swans bound for Chesapeake Bay make some tremendous long-distance flights, flying both day and night, sometimes nonstop for 1,000 miles. Reports from airplane pilots on the altitude of migrating whistling swans between Minneapolis and Chesapeake Bay show the swans at heights

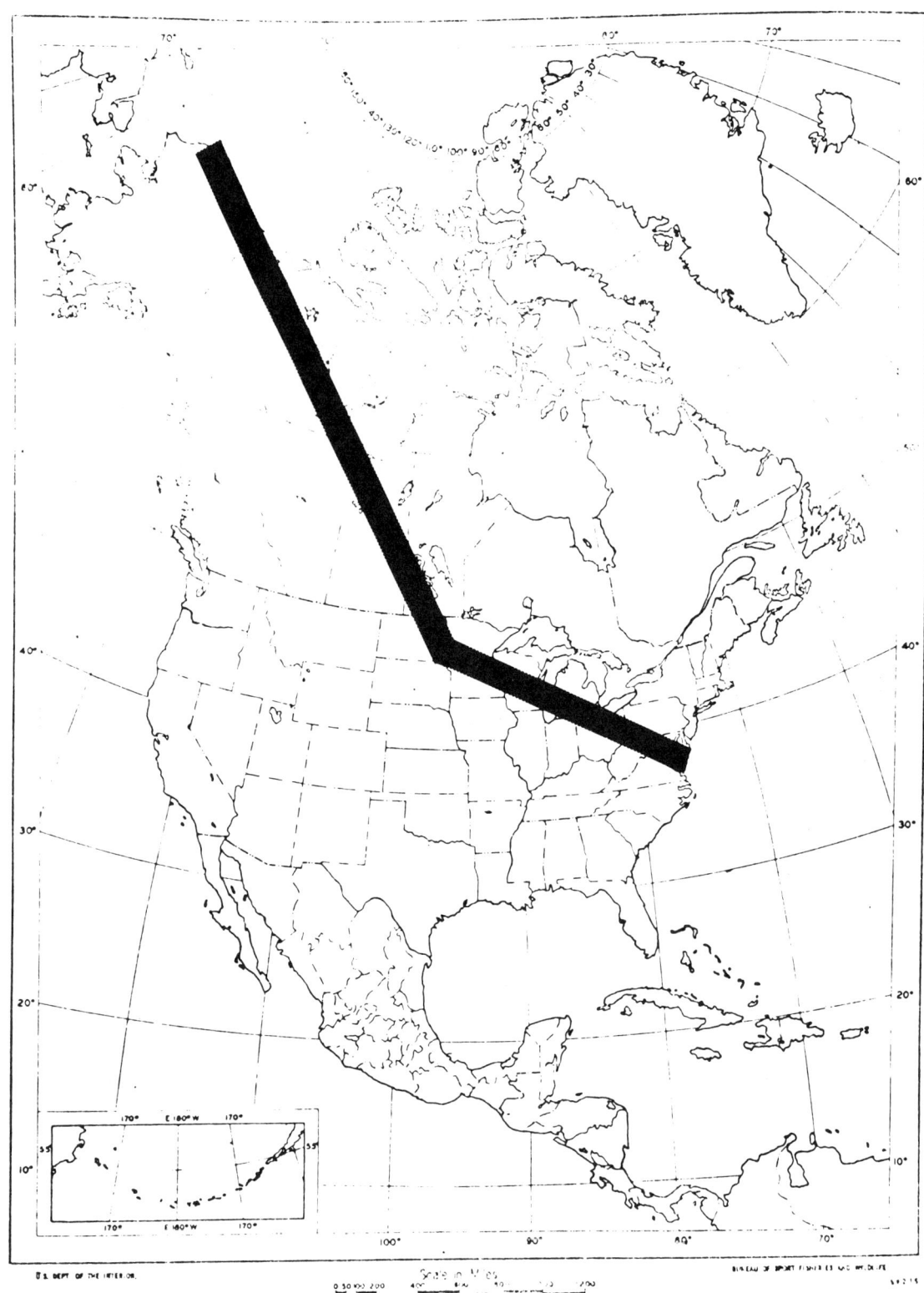

Fig. 112. Main migration corridor of the whistling swan from breeding grounds in northern Alaska and northwestern Canadian tundra to Chesapeake Bay wintering area (from Palmer, 1975; and Bellrose, 1976).

ranging from 2,000 to 6,000 feet (Fig. 113). Most swans leave the breeding grounds by late September and early October, arriving at Chesapeake Bay in late October and November. There were only six swans at Blackwater Refuge on November 3, 1976, but by the 19th, there were over 100.

In the Chesapeake wintering area swans are generally restricted to fairly extensive open brackish waters no more than five feet deep. The largest percentage of the Bay population has usually been centered in the lower Chester River, Eastern Bay, lower Choptank River, and the Miles River. Smaller numbers also occur in other sections of the central Chesapeake area, including the larger ponds of the fresh and brackish estuarine bay marshes in southern Dorchester County, and freshwater impoundments of Blackwater Refuge.

The larger concentrations have usually been in places where submerged aquatic plants have been abundant. The Susquehanna Flats near the head of the Bay were formerly an important wintering area. However, in recent years, probably due to pollution and turbidity, submerged plants have been in short supply in that area and other favored feeding grounds. This may be the reason whistling swans sometimes shift their foraging activities to winter wheat fields, soybean stubble, and other closely cropped upland fields near estuaries. This recent change in feeding behavior seems to have brought larger numbers of swans closer to the Blackwater area. In the past few winters, flocks of several thousand have been observed in upland fields near Church Creek (Fig. 114). Sometimes they are associated with Canada geese and a few snow geese in these fields.

Fig. 113. Migrating swans fly very high, often 2,000-6,000 feet, and during a sustained flight may average 50 miles per hour.

Looking back 20 years to the 1950s, Stewart and Manning (35) listed several species of submerged aquatic plants and several species of mollusks as the principal food of whistling swans in the Chesapeake Bay wintering grounds. Wild celery was the most important food in fresh estuarine waters, while in brackish estuarine areas (Fig. 115), the more important foods were represented by widgeongrass and sago pondweed, in addition to two species of thin-shelled mollusks, the long (soft-shelled) clam and one known as Baltic macoma. Although wild celery is scarce in the Bay area today, sizable beds occur in a few areas, one of which is Savannah Lake on

Fig. 114. Whistling swans in stubble field near Church Creek, January 1976. Possibly because of a shortage of submerged aquatic vegetation in Chesapeake Bay estuaries in recent years, they sometimes shift their feeding activity to upland fields—winter wheat, corn, and soybean stubble.

Fig. 115. Whistling swans and other waterfowl resting and feeding in estuary. Submerged aquatic foods of swans in this habitat include widgeongrass, pondweeds, and mollusks.

Elliott Island, in southern Dorchester County. Each winter swans are frequently seen utilizing this resource. In the shallow estuarine marsh ponds of the Blackwater marsh, swans still find some widgeongrass, sago pondweed, and muskgrass.

The Baltic macoma clam (see Fig. 78) is still an important food. Mike Haramis of the U.S. Fish and Wildlife Service reported swans feeding on this clam in December 1976, near the mouth of the Choptank River some seven miles north of Blackwater.

As indicated, some of the feeding is now in stubble fields in the uplands. In January 1976, while John W. Taylor, the waterfowl artist, and I were watching a flock of field-feeding swans near Church Creek, our binoculars "picked up" a bird with a red plastic neck collar. We knew that this bird was one of many marked by Dr. William Sladen and associates, of Johns Hopkins University, who had been working on the nesting grounds in the Yukon Territory. Dr. Sladen is charting the movements of swans to and from Chesapeake Bay wintering grounds and arctic breeding grounds, using an internationally coordinated marking system (36). The color-coded neck bands identify an individual bird from 300 yards with a spotting scope. I saw two "marked" swans at Blackwater on November 19, 1976, with black neck collars bearing the numbers F111 and F118. Black collars are placed on birds in the Middle Atlantic States. Both birds were "marked" at Blackwater in 1973.

The winter stay at Blackwater and the rest of the Chesapeake Bay Country ends by March, and by the middle of the month, flocks often numbering a hundred or so take off for northern breeding grounds.

In migrating, swans fly in a "V" like Canada geese. One flock that I observed was accompanied by a small flock of ring-billed gulls, a smaller species, flying in a "V" within the larger "V" of the swans. I have never heard of this before. Swans migrating to breeding grounds fly by way of the Great Lakes, which is also the route of ring-billed gulls.

In the spring of 1973, Dr. Sladen followed by aircraft, five of eight migrating swans fitted with radio tracking transmitters, from Chesapeake Bay to the Great Lakes. All eight were relocated in the Detroit area; six of eight were tracked and relocated in Minnesota and/or North Dakota; then two were tracked from North Dakota to Saskatchewan.

Dr. Sladen's study of migration and movements of Chesapeake Bay swans is most interesting and important. The more we know about the annual cycle of the whistling swan, the better we can manage the population. Blackwater and other refuges located within the range of the whistling swan are a part of the management program.

Winter of '77

The winter of 1977 was one of some note. However, the National Weather Service, which has been keeping official records since the 1870s, reports that there were seven winters that were colder. The coldest was the winter of 1917-18, with average Fahrenheit temperatures of 25.8 degrees for the months of December and January combined. The average for those two months in 1976-77 was 30.5 degrees. By late January and early February in the winter of 1977, the Chesapeake Bay from about Tangier Island north was completely frozen. From the high point on the Bay Bridge (Maryland), the solidly frozen Bay looked like a scene from the arctic region and for several weeks there was very little ship traffic up the Bay into Baltimore.

Fig. 116. Frozen needlerush marsh along Beaverdam Creek, about three miles west of Blackwater National Wildlife Refuge, February 10, 1977.

How does wildlife of the Chesapeake Bay Country adjust to a winter when the Bay, rivers, creeks, and marshes are frozen solid (Fig. 116)? Canada geese, whistling swans, and some of the dabbling or marsh ducks that alternate feeding sites between

Fig. 117. Whistling swans and a few ducks standing on the frozen Choptank River near Cambridge, Maryland, February 10, 1977. Residents of the town were probably feeding the group during the freeze-up. However, at the time many swans were feeding in corn and soybean stubbles between Cambridge and Blackwater.

Fig. 118. Canada geese standing on the ice at Blackwater National Wildlife Refuge during the winter freeze of 1977. The geese would feed in nearby grain stubble fields and return to the Refuge to get a drink in an open water hole and to loaf.

Fig. 119. Canvasbacks and whistling swans keeping open a small section of the frozen Choptank River near Cambridge, Dorchester County, Maryland. Note edge of ice in background, February 10, 1977.

Fig. 120. This photograph, made about ten miles north of Blackwater along the Choptank River in January 1977, shows a hole in the ice kept open by a small raft of canvasbacks. A close look will show that most of the canvasbacks are asleep, apparently unconcerned about the presence of a bald eagle perched on the edge of the ice nearby. Bald eagles seldom capture healthy ducks, preferring the easier method of preying on sick, wounded, or dead birds. The eagle in this photograph was feeding on a bufflehead. Photograph by Mike Haramis, U.S. Fish and Wildlife Service.

corn and soybean stubble fields and shallow waters and marshes, fare just about as well as under normal winter conditions by generally staying in the fields. From time to time they return to a watering hole and then stand around on the ice (Figs. 117 and 118).

Most diving ducks have to seek open water farther south. Occasionally a few that were in an area before the freeze will keep a small spot open if they are provided with grain by the local people (Figs. 119 and 120). If the hole is large enough, they may dive for a few clams. Matt Perry of the U.S. Fish and Wildlife Service told me that in early February 1977, during the height of the Bay freeze-up, there were an estimated 40,000 canvasbacks in the lower Potomac, Rappahannock, and York Rivers.

Fig. 121. The great blue heron is the only member of the heron-egret family that regularly winters at Blackwater. On the December 21, 1973 Christmas count, 139 were recorded in southern Dorchester County. During the exceptionally cold winter of 1977, six were found dead at Blackwater Refuge. Photograph by Luther Goldman, U.S. Fish and Wildlife Service.

Most songbirds fare better during a long frozen winter than the water birds. The myrtle or yellow-rumped warbler is a good example. At Blackwater this resourceful winter resident from farther north feeds on wax myrtle and poison ivy berries, and even on the sap exuding from wells or shallow pits dug into the bark of maple trees by the yellow-bellied sapsucker.

In the Blackwater and nearby Elliott Island areas of southern Dorchester County, some forms of wildlife suffered greatly. An early indication of the effects of the severe winter on wildlife was demonstrated by the southern Dorchester Christmas bird count of December 31, 1976, when only 111 species were noted compared to 132 species on the December 31, 1975 count.

A species such as the belted kingfisher, that depends totally upon fish for food and normally winters in the area, was frozen out and by late winter had to move on. The great blue heron, another fish eater and usually a common winter resident (Fig. 121), will seek alternate foods such as meadow mice and small birds that live in the marshes. The great blue is a "tough" bird, but six dead ones were found during the '77 freeze by Guy Willey, biologist at Blackwater Refuge. On February 10, I saw only four all day at Blackwater where usually I see about 25 at that time of the year.

Some animals get desperate during such adverse conditions. Bill Julian, manager at Blackwater, told me that some muskrats that could not get into the frozen substrate to feed on their favorite food (the rootstocks of Olney three-square), were known to be feeding on other muskrats that were caught in traps.

Probably few mammals suffered as much as the exotic nutria, the South American furbearer that has been doing fairly well in southern Dorchester marshes for the past 30 years. However, the winter of 1977 had a devastating effect on the nutria population, as observed by Bill Burton at Elliott Island on January 19th, and reported in his column in the Baltimore *Evening Sun* (37):

"The marsh above here is cold and bleak with little sign of life anywhere.

"Oystermen and fishermen are icebound, most waterfowl are gone, muskrats are holed up, and most trappers are idle.

"There are some things in life in which it pays to be atop the heap. But being a nutria, a rodent imported from South America, in the current weather isn't one of them. The furbearers on the top are usually the ones that, as they say, 'wake up dead.'

"The nutria has not fully adapted to severe weather. While the winterwise muskrats retreat to their relatively comfy dens when things freeze up and the mercury plummets close to zero, the nutria spend the night in their instinctive way.

"They platform, and I saw the result of platforming not far from the Fishing Bay Wildlife Management Area. Makes one feel sorry for the pesky furbearers that are competing with the more valuable native muskrat for habitat.

"Platforming is simply balling up on the frozen marsh. These king size guinea pigs, some which weigh a dozen pounds or more, pile up to utilize group warmth. Those on the bottom of the heap survive. The last ones to platform are exposed to the cold—and during near zero nights they perish. The carrion eaters find food on the marsh these days. It's nature's way, but so cruel."

By the second week in February there was a break in the weather with high daily temperatures in the 50s for a few days, and some of the narrow creeks with a swift tidal current were beginning to open a little. As I looked over the Blackwater marsh on February 10, there was already a sign of spring, perhaps the first, and one that I note every year at that time: male red-winged blackbirds holding forth from poles stuck into the marsh by muskrat trappers (Fig. 122). The redwings had begun to advertise their territorial rights through song and display as they would continue to do throughout the next four or five months. For the redwing, spring had arrived!

Fig. 122. Red-winged blackbirds, harbingers of spring in tidal marshes of Dorchester County, use the poles set out by muskrat trappers from which to proclaim their territorial rights in early February and through the spring. Illustration by John W. Taylor.

Rare Occurrences of Birds at Blackwater

Any area as attractive to birds as Blackwater is going to provide a lot of interesting records. Such rarities occur because some birds get off course in their migrations, customarily wander north of their breeding range in late summer, are driven inland by coastal storms, and some from the far north are forced south because of a shortage of the staple food supply. Birders spend less time at Blackwater in summer when it is hot and mosquitoes and flies are biting, so most of the unusual sightings are made in other seasons. However, I suspect that if more effort were spent in late summer, a time of postnesting season wandering of birds, more unusual records might be made than at any other period.

Fortunately, many rarities remain in the area for several days—long enough for other birdwatchers to be alerted. If an original sighting is substantiated by other persons, the record has more credibility, for there are more "doubting Thomases" among birdwatchers than in any other element of society.

For a new bird to be admitted to the State list, according to Stewart and Robbins, authors of *Birds of Maryland and the District of Columbia* (4), the following three prerequisites have to be met: 1) a specimen preserved (usually in museum collections); 2) a satisfactory photograph taken; 3) or three or more reliable sight observations made. In reference to these criteria, I recall the time Matt Perry and I saw a red-cockaded woodpecker near Bowie, Prince Georges County, well north of its range. Fortunately we were "protected" since we obtained an identifiable color photograph of the bird as it was climbing up the trunk of a Virginia or scrub pine (also identifiable), a tree that does not occur at Blackwater (in the range of the red-cockade), and is virtually outside of the range of this southern woodpecker. Furthermore, the film processor dated the color photograph.

Most of the rarities seen at Blackwater have been larger birds—swallow-tailed kite, fulvous tree duck, gull-billed tern, black-necked stilt, gyrfalcon, white pelican, and several others. Smaller rarities, songbird types, especially various warblers that normally migrate to the tropics in winter, occasionally are reported on Christmas bird counts.

Any rarity is exciting to the birder and is often publicized in the local newspaper. If unusual enough, a report may be published in an ornithological journal.

Sometimes a rare bird sighting happens under the most ideal circumstances. On May 20, 1976, I had just sat down to talk with Peter J. Van Huizen in his front yard, a few miles north of Blackwater, and as we settled back facing the open country, we could hardly believe what we were seeing when we observed a swallow-tailed kite (Fig. 123) heading in our direction at about 100 feet in altitude. Van and I both knew the bird from our years in the deep South where they occur in the summer-half of the year. The only area where they are still common is in the Everglades

Fig. 123. The swallow-tailed kite has been reported in Maryland seven times. In the United States this species is common only in the Everglades region of Florida. A few nest along the South Atlantic Coast as far north as the Santee River in South Carolina. A close look will reveal that the bird pictured above has a frog in its talons (note frog's legs). Photograph by Noel Snyder.

region of south Florida. A few nest as far north along the Atlantic Coast as the delta region of the Santee River in South Carolina. But over the years we know of at least seven that have come up the Coast as far as Maryland. Three were seen in the latter part of the last century and four in this century. Approximately four years prior to our 1976 record, Larry Dunkeson and Bill Julian saw one at Blackwater Refuge on May 31 (1972) (38). Its picture appeared on the cover of *Maryland Birdlife*, September 1972. None have been known to nest in Maryland.

A gyrfalcon sighted at Blackwater in the fall of 1972 is one of the rarest birds ever recorded in the State. This arctic species is occasionally seen along the New England coast and states bordering Canada. A note of its occurrence at Blackwater was mentioned in *Maryland Birdlife* (39), and reported as follows:

Fig. 124. Portrait of a peregrine. The peregrine falcon, once well known to ornithologists in Maryland, is now on the U.S. Fish and Wildlife Service's rare and endangered list. Six have been seen on Southern Dorchester County Christmas Bird Counts in the last 30 years; and one occasionally passes through Blackwater during spring or fall migration.

"The rarity of the period was a Gyrfalcon, a new species for Maryland's Hypothetical List. It was discovered on November 30 at Blackwater Refuge (Refuge Manager William Julian) and was subsequently sighted on Dec. 3 (Robert Hahn), Dec. 4 (identification confirmed by Carl W. Carlson), Dec. 5 (Paul G. DuMont), Dec. 6 (Rowlett), and Dec. 8 (Philip DuMont). Unfortunately, no one was able to obtain photographs, so the Gyrfalcon can not be admitted to the official State List."

A second gyrfalcon was seen in the Blackwater area by Bill Julian on March 26, 1977. It was perched on a muskrat house.

The peregrine falcon, now on the rare and endangered species list (Fig. 124), is occasionally sighted at Blackwater. At one time this noble bird nested on the cliffs of some of our western Maryland mountains. I can remember when a pair nested year after year at Harpers Ferry in the 1930s and '40s.

The white pelican of the West, not so well-known to us as the brown pelican of the South Atlantic area, has been reported in Maryland five times. The fifth Maryland record was of a bird reported by G. Wallace Stewart at Blackwater Refuge on February 28, 1970 (40). White pelicans nest in the Dakotas, on islands in Great Salt Lake, and in the western Prairie Provinces of Canada. Some of them winter along the Louisiana and Texas coasts.

Of special interest to me was the occurrence of a fulvous tree duck at Blackwater in the late fall of 1975. I did not see the bird, but I know the species well from my research of it in the Louisiana Gulf Coast marshes and rice fields. The appearance at Blackwater was the fourth record for Maryland. The first sighting was by Charlotte Hoover in the summer of 1960 at Ocean City.

The tree duck is a unique bird, differing decidedly in form and habits from its better-known relatives (Fig. 125). It is long-legged and long-necked and mostly of tropical and semitropical distribution. The plumage of both sexes is similar. Tree ducks fly with feet trailing behind, neck outstretched and slightly drooping, and in no set formation, rather in a loose line or disorganized group.

The name whistling duck has been proposed for this species, because its whistle-like call is more characteristic of the bird than its arboreal affinities. Other species of tree ducks do perch in trees and nest in tree cavities, but not so the fulvous tree duck. In Louisiana most of them nest in the cultivated rice fields.

The fulvous tree duck probably has the most remarkable geographical distribution of any bird in the world. It is locally fairly common along the Louisiana and contiguous Texas coast, and the San Joaquin Valley of California. Its range also includes parts of Mexico, Central and South America, East Africa, Madagascar, India, Ceylon, and Burma. This is an extraordinary example of discontinuous distribution.

Prior to 1960, the fulvous tree ducks in our country were restricted to Louisiana, Texas and California. Then for some unexplained reason, they began showing up in Florida, and in small numbers along the South Atlantic and Middle Atlantic Coasts, but none have nested in the new part of their range. It is still a "red-letter day" when one is seen this far north of the Gulf Coast.

There also are the exotics that have shown up at Blackwater, the Egyptian goose, Stanley (paradise) crane, flamingo, and others. Apparently they are not likely to be added to the State list even if they satisfy the requirements, as they probably escaped from a zoo or someone had them in captivity and decided to release them thinking that a wildlife refuge would be the appropriate place for deposition.

Fig. 125. A fulvous tree duck, long-legged and long-necked bird mainly of subtropical and tropical distribution, was seen at Blackwater Refuge during the fall of 1975. It has been observed in the State on at least four other occasions. A few nest in the Gulf Coast region of Louisiana and Texas.

Fig. 126. Glossy ibis with ribbed mussel attached to its foot. Bill Julian, who photographed this bird, was able to splinter the mussel with a well-placed rifle shot that relieved the ibis of its burden without injury to the foot.

Fig. 127. "Civilisation." Sometimes someone throws a beer or softdrink can separator into a pond or marsh. A duck, goose or other waterbird that dabbles, tips-up, or dives for food may surface with one of these plastic collars around its neck. I have seen photographs of other birds in this predicament, and have seen a herring gull so encumbered flying over Chesapeake Bay. This goose was photographed at Blackwater Refuge, but may have picked up the plastic collar during one of its trips away from the Refuge. Photograph courtesy of William H. Julian, Blackwater National Wildlife Refuge.

Two species that were listed as rare or casual in Maryland when *Birds of Maryland and the District of Columbia* was published in 1958, are now common spring and summer residents in the general area of Blackwater. The cattle egret extended its range from South America to the United States in the early 1940s; the glossy ibis, a common breeding bird of our southern coastal states, is rapidly expanding its range northward along the Atlantic Coast. Both nest in mixed heronries or rookeries on Barren, Bloodsworth, and some of the other Chesapeake Bay islands opposite Dorchester and Somerset Counties.

Bill Julian, Refuge Manager at Blackwater, made an unusual series of photographs of a glossy ibis that had a ribbed mussel attached to its foot (Fig. 126). Bill was able to splinter the mussel with a well-placed shot that relieved the ibis of its burden without injury to its foot. Another unique photograph by Julian is reproduced in Fig. 127.

But of the approximately 850 species of birds in North America, there are none that I would rather see at Blackwater than the red-cockaded woodpecker. Once a resident bird in limited numbers, it is now all but extirpated in Maryland. If someone is lucky enough to locate another red-cockade in Dorchester County or any other place in the State, I would hope to be the first birdwatcher standing in line to get a glimpse of this extremely rare Maryland bird.

APPENDICES

APPENDIX I

Southern Dorchester County Christmas Bird Count

30-Year Summary, 1947-1976

Species	No. Years Obs.	Highest No.	Lowest No.
common loon	6	3	0
horned grebe	28	304	0
pied-billed grebe	23	20	0
gannet	1	1	0
great blue heron	30	139	11
little blue heron	1	1	0
great egret	15	8	0
snowy egret	3	2	0
Louisiana heron	1	1	0
black-crowned night heron	24	28	0
American bittern	24	7	0
glossy ibis	2	1	0
whistling swan	28	2,770	0
Canada goose	30	46,800	1,570
Atlantic brant	4	1,300	0
white-fronted goose	1	1	0
snow goose	28	3,014	0
mallard	30	16,650	70
black duck	30	10,125	160
gadwall	22	556	0
pintail	29	3,625	0
green-winged teal	28	1,170	0
blue-winged teal	20	39	0
European wigeon	2	1	0
American wigeon	30	1,425	1
northern shoveler	18	60	0
wood duck	6	5	0
redhead	23	865	0
ring-necked duck	14	3,500	0
canvasback	29	9,090	0
scaup (greater and lesser)	28	4,491	0
common goldeneye	30	1,200	1
bufflehead	29	561	0
old-squaw	24	375	0
white-winged scoter	6	50	0
surf scoter	7	22	0
black scoter	4	4	0
ruddy duck	25	1,500	0

Species	No. Years Obs.	Highest No.	Lowest No.
hooded merganser	24	95	0
common merganser	27	1,171	0
red-breasted merganser	23	88	0
turkey vulture	29	412	0
black vulture	16	20	0
goshawk	2	1	0
sharp-shinned hawk	28	8	0
Cooper's hawk	23	7	0
red-tailed hawk	30	30	2
red-shouldered hawk	30	18	1
rough-legged hawk	30	27	1
golden eagle	15	3	0
bald eagle	29	36	0
marsh hawk	30	91	19
peregrine falcon	4	2	0
merlin	7	1	0
American kestrel	30	38	1
bobwhite	29	217	0
wild turkey	1	1	0
king rail	14	32	0
clapper rail	12	9	0
Virginia rail	28	155	0
sora	9	4	0
black rail	1	1	0
American coot	18	58	0
killdeer	29	198	0
black-bellied plover	1	1	0
American woodcock	27	25	0
common snipe	28	97	0
greater yellowlegs	24	26	0
lesser yellowlegs	14	15	0
least sandpiper	1	1	0
dunlin	12	444	0
dowitcher (spp.)	2	1	0
semipalmated sandpiper	1	7	0
western sandpiper	1	1	0
sanderling	1	2	0
great black-backed gull	26	28	0
herring gull	30	515	18
ring-billed gull	30	905	15
laughing gull	3	1	0
Bonaparte's gull	1	2	0
Forster's tern	1	1	0
rock dove	3	9	0
mourning dove	28	747	0

Appendix I

Species	No. Years Obs.	Highest No.	Lowest No.
barn owl	18	10	0
screech owl	22	24	0
great horned owl	29	47	0
barred owl	24	5	0
long-eared owl	4	13	0
short-eared owl	24	17	0
saw-whet owl	4	2	0
belted kingfisher	29	65	0
common flicker	30	169	5
pileated woodpecker	28	28	0
red-bellied woodpecker	29	66	0
red-headed woodpecker	3	1	0
yellow-bellied sapsucker	8	3	0
hairy woodpecker	30	37	1
downy woodpecker	30	116	14
red-cockaded woodpecker	1	1	0
eastern phoebe	7	2	0
horned lark	22	152	0
tree swallow	11	1,255	0
blue jay	30	372	1
common crow	30	11,870	258
fish crow	21	76	0
black-capped chickadee	4	7	0
Carolina chickadee	30	332	28
tufted titmouse	30	92	5
white-breasted nuthatch	19	34	0
red-breasted nuthatch	13	34	0
brown-headed nuthatch	30	482	23
brown creeper	29	51	0
house wren	11	6	0
winter wren	30	39	2
Carolina wren	30	242	3
long-billed marsh wren	28	127	0
short-billed marsh wren	25	164	0
mockingbird	30	109	1
gray catbird	27	24	0
brown thrasher	26	29	0
robin	30	2,570	1
hermit thrush	28	64	0
Swainson's thrush	1	1	0
eastern bluebird	28	255	0
golden-crowned kinglet	30	252	21
ruby-crowned kinglet	28	148	0
water pipit	21	228	0
cedar waxwing	21	182	0

Species	No. Years Obs.	Highest No.	Lowest No.
northern shrike	1	1	0
loggerhead shrike	25	7	0
starling	30	3,835	60
black and white warbler	1	1	0
orange-crowned warbler	1	1	0
Nashville warbler	1	1	0
yellow-rumped warbler	30	6,500	122
pine warbler	13	5	0
palm warbler	12	3	0
yellowthroat	21	13	0
house sparrow	30	670	30
eastern meadowlark	30	633	13
red-winged blackbird	30	500,000	1,060
rusty blackbird	23	58	0
boat-tailed grackle	15	475	0
common grackle	30	150,000	2
brown-headed cowbird	26	2,095	0
cardinal	30	357	22
evening grosbeak	14	400	0
purple finch	20	20	0
house finch	2	36	0
pine grosbeak	1	2	0
common redpoll	1	2	0
pine siskin	14	258	0
American goldfinch	29	548	0
red crossbill	3	223	0
white-winged crossbill	2	35	0
rufous-sided towhee	30	165	2
Savannah sparrow	30	239	7
sharp-tailed sparrow	18	11	0
seaside sparrow	7	7	0
vesper sparrow	16	8	0
Bachman's sparrow	1	1	0
dark-eyed junco	30	315	8
tree sparrow	29	33	0
chipping sparrow	9	10	0
field sparrow	30	246	9
white-crowned sparrow	6	23	0
white-throated sparrow	30	1,550	83
fox sparrow	28	43	0
swamp sparrow	30	1,271	86
song sparrow	30	869	85
Lapland longspur	1	1	0
snow bunting	1	1	0

APPENDIX II

Common and Scientific Names of Birds

bittern, American *(Botaurus lentiginosus)*
    least *(Ixobrychus exilis)*
blackbird, red-winged *(Agelaius phoeniceus)*
    rusty *(Euphagus carolinus)*
bluebird, eastern *(Sialia sialis)*
bobwhite *(Colinus virginianus)*
bufflehead *(Bucephala albeola)*
bunting, snow *(Plectrophenax nivalis)*

canvasback *(Aythya valisineria)*
cardinal *(Cardinalis cardinalis)*
catbird, gray *(Dumetella carolinensis)*
chickadee, black-capped *(Parus atricapillus)*
    Carolina *(Parus carolinensis)*
chuck-will's-widow *(Caprimulgus carolinensis)*
coot, American *(Fulica americana)*
cowbird, brown-headed *(Molothrus ater)*
crane, Stanley or paradise
    (Anthropoides paradisea)
creeper, brown *(Certhia familiaris)*
crossbill, red *(Loxia curvirostra)*
    white-winged *(Loxia leucoptera)*
crow, common *(Corvus brachyrhynchos)*
    fish *(Corvus ossifragus)*

dove, mourning *(Zenaida macroura)*
    rock *(Columba livia)*
dowitcher *(Limnodromus sp.)*
duck, black *(Anas rubripes)*
    fulvous tree *(Dendrocygna bicolor)*
    ring-necked *(Aythya collaris)*
    ruddy *(Oxyura jamaicensis)*
    wood *(Aix sponsa)*
dunlin *(Erolia alpina)*

eagle, bald *(Haliaeetus leucocephalus)*
    golden *(Aquila chrysaetos)*
egret, cattle *(Bubulcus ibis)*
    great *(Casmerodius albus)*
    snowy *(Egretta thula)*

falcon, peregrine *(Falco peregrinus)*
finch, house *(Carpodacus mexicanus)*
    purple *(Carpodacus purpureus)*
flamingo *(Phoenicopterus ruber)*
flicker, common *(Colaptes auratus)*
flycatcher, great crested *(Myiarchus crinitus)*

gadwall *(Anas strepera)*
gannet *(Morus bassanus)*
gnatcatcher, blue-gray *(Polioptela caerulea)*
goldeneye, common *(Bucephala clangula)*
goldfinch, American *(Spinus tristis)*
goose, Canada *(Branta canadensis)*
    Egyptian *(Alopochen aegyptiacus)*
    greater snow *(Chen caerulescens atlanticus)*
    lesser snow *(Chen caerulescens caerulescens)*

goose, white-fronted *(Anser albifrons)*
goshawk *(Accipter gentilis)*
grackle, boat-tailed *(Quiscalus major)*
    common or bronzed
        (Quiscalus quiscula versicolor)
    common or purple
        (Quiscalus quiscula stonei)
grebe, horned *(Podiceps auritus)*
    pied-billed *(Podilymbus podiceps)*
grosbeak, evening *(Guiraca caerulea)*
    pine *(Pinicola enucleator)*
gull, Bonaparte's *(Larus philadelphia)*
    great black-backed *(Larus marinus)*
    herring *(Larus argentatus)*
    laughing *(Larus atricilla)*
    ring-billed *(Larus delawarensis)*
gyrfalcon *(Falco rusticolus)*

hawk, Cooper's *(Accipter cooperii)*
    marsh *(Circus cyaneus)*
    red-shouldered *(Buteo lineatus)*
    red-tailed *(Buteo jamaicensis)*
    rough-legged *(Buteo lagopus)*
    sharp-shinned *(Accipter striatus)*
    sparrow *(Falco sparvarius)*
heron, black-crowned night
    (Nycticorax nycticorax)
    great blue *(Ardea herodias)*
    little blue *(Florida caerulea)*
    Louisiana *(Hydranassa tricolor)*
hummingbird, ruby-throated
    (Archilochus colubris)

ibis, glossy *(Plegadis falcinellus)*

jay, blue *(Cyanocitta cristata)*
junco, dark-eyed *(Junco hyemalis)*

kestrel *(Falco sparvarius)*
killdeer *(Charadrius vociferus)*
kingbird, eastern *(Tyrannus tyrannus)*
kingfisher, belted *(Megaceryle alcyon)*
kinglet, golden-crowned *(Regulus satrapa)*
    ruby-crowned *(Regulus calendula)*
kite, swallow-tailed *(Elanoides forficatus)*

lark, horned *(Eremophila alpestris)*
longspur, Lapland *(Calcarius lapponicus)*
loon, common *(Gavia immer)*

mallard *(Anas platyrhynchos)*
meadowlark, eastern *(Sturnella magna)*
merganser, common *(Mergus merganser)*
    hooded *(Mergus cucullatus)*
    red-breasted *(Mergus serrator)*
merlin *(Falco columbarius)*
mockingbird *(Mimus polyglottos)*

nuthatch, brown-headed *(Sitta pusilla)*
    red-breasted *(Sitta canadensis)*
    white-breasted *(Sitta carolinensis)*
old-squaw *(Clangula hyemalis)*
oriole, northern or Baltimore
    (Icterus galbula galbula)
  northern or Bullock's
    (Icterus galbula bullockii)
osprey *(Pandion haliaetus)*
ovenbird *(Seiurus aurocapillus)*
owl, barn *(Tyto alba)*
  barred *(Strix varia)*
  great horned *(Bubo virginianus)*
  long-eared *(Asio otus)*
  saw-whet *(Aegolius acadicus)*
  screech *(Otus asio)*
  short-eared *(Asio flammeus)*
  snowy *(Nyctea scandiaca)*
pelican, white *(Pelecanus erythrorhynchos)*
pewee, eastern wood *(Contopus virens)*
phoebe *(Sayornis phoebe)*
pigeon, passenger *(Ectopistes migratorius)*
pintail *(Anas acuta)*
pipit, water *(Anthus spinoletta)*
plover, black-bellied *(Squatarola squatarola)*
  semipalmated *(Charadrius semipalmatus)*
rail, black *(Laterallus jamaicensis)*
  clapper *(Rallus longirostris)*
  king *(Rallus elegans)*
  Virginia *(Rallus limicola)*
redhead *(Aythya americana)*
redpoll, common *(Acanthis flammea)*
robin *(Turdus migratorius)*
sanderling *(Crocethia alba)*
sandpiper, least *(Erolia minutilla)*
sandpiper, semipalmated *(Calidris pusilla)*
  western *(Calidris mauri)*
  white-rumped *(Calidris fuscicollis)*
sapsucker, yellow-bellied *(Sphyrapicus varius)*
scaup, greater *(Aythya marila)*
  lesser *(Aythya affinis)*
scoter, black *(Melanitta nigra)*
  surf *(Melanitta perspicillata)*
  white-winged *(Melanitta fusca)*
shoveler, northern *(Anas clypeata)*
shrike, loggerhead *(Lanius ludovicianus)*
  northern *(Lanius excubitor)*
siskin, pine *(Spinus pinus)*
snipe, common *(Capella gallinago)*
sora *(Porzana carolina)*
sparrow, Bachman's *(Aimophila aestivalis)*
  chipping *(Spizella passerina)*
  field *(Spizella pusilla)*
  fox *(Passerella iliaca)*
  house *(Passer domesticus)*
  Savannah *(Passerculus sandwichensis)*
  seaside *(Ammospiza maritima)*
  sharp-tailed *(Ammospiza caudacuta)*
  song *(Melospiza melodia)*
  swamp *(Melospiza georgiana)*
  tree *(Spizella arborea)*
sparrow, vesper *(Pooecetes gramineus)*
  white-crowned *(Zonotrichia leucophrys)*
  white-throated *(Zonotrichia albicollis)*
starling *(Sturnus vulgaris)*
stilt, black-necked *(Himantopus mexicanus)*
swallow, tree *(Iridoprocne bicolor)*
swan, whistling *(Olar columbianus)*
tanager, summer *(Piranga rubra)*
teal, blue-winged *(Anas discors)*
  green-winged *(Anas crecca)*
tern, Forster's *(Sterna forsteri)*
  gull-billed *(Gelochelidon nilotica)*
thrasher, brown *(Toxostoma rufum)*
thrush, hermit *(Catharus guttatus)*
  Swainson's *(Catharus ustulatus)*
  wood *(Hylocichla mustelina)*
timberdoodle, or American woodcock
  (Philohela minor)
titmouse, tufted *(Parus bicolor)*
towhee, rufous-sided *(Pipilo erythrophthalmus)*
turkey, wild *(Meleagris gallopavo)*
vireo, white-eyed *(Vireo griseus)*
vulture, black *(Coragyps atratus)*
  turkey *(Cathartes aura)*
warbler, black and white *(Mniotilta varia)*
  Nashville *(Vermivora ruficapilla)*
  orange-crowned *(Vermivora celata)*
warbler, palm *(Dendroica palmarum)*
  pine *(Dendroica pinus)*
  yellow-rumped *(Dendroica coronata)*
  yellow-throated *(Dendroica dominica)*
waterthrush, northern *(Seiurus noveboracensis)*
waxwing, cedar *(Bombycilla cedrorum)*
wigeon, American *(Anas americana)*
  European *(Anas penelope)*
willet *(Catoptrophorus semipalmatus)*
woodcock, American *(Philohela minor)*
woodpecker, downy *(Picoides pubescens)*
  hairy *(Picoides villosus)*
  pileated *(Dendrocopus pileatus)*
  red-bellied *(Melanerpes carolinus)*
  red-cockaded *(Picoides borealis)*
  red-headed *(Melanerpes erythrocephalus)*
wren, Carolina *(Thryothorus ludovicianus)*
  house *(Troglodytes aedon)*
  long-billed marsh *(Cistothorus palustris)*
  short-billed marsh *(Cistothorus platensis)*
  winter *(Troglodytes troglodytes)*
yellowlegs, greater *(Tringa melanoleuca)*
  lesser *(Tringa flavipes)*
yellowthroat, common *(Geothlypis trichas)*

Appendix II

Common and Scientific Names of Mammals

deer, white-tailed *(Odocoileus virginianus)*
fox, gray *(Urocyon cinereoargenteus)*
    red *(Vulpes fulva)*
mink *(Mustela vison)*
mole, eastern *(Scalopus aquaticus)*
mouse, house *(Mus musculus)*
    wood *(Peromyscus sp.)*
muskrat, Virginia *(Ondatra zibethicus)*
nutria *(Myocaster coypus)*
otter *(Lutra canadensis)*

raccoon *(Procyon lotor)*
rat, brown *(Rattus sp.)*
    rice *(Oryzomys palustris)*
shrew, long-tailed *(Sorex dispar)*
    short-tailed *(Blarina brevicauda)*
squirrel, Delmarva fox *(Sciurus niger cinereus)*
    eastern fox *(Sciurus niger vulpinus)*
    eastern gray *(Sciurus carolinensis)*
    flying *(Glaucomys volans)*
vole, meadow *(Microtus pennsylvanicus)*

Common and Scientific Names of Other Animals

beetle, crawling water *(Haliplus fasciatus)*
    water scavenger *(Hydrophilus sp.)*
boatman, water *(Corixa sp.)*
carp *(Cyprinus carpio)*
clam, long ("soft-shelled") *(Mya arenaria)*
    macoma *(Macoma balthica)*
crab, blue *(Callinectes sapidus)*
crayfish *(Cambarus sp.)*
dragonfly *(Anisoptera)*

killifishes *(Poecilidae)*
minnow, top *(Fundulus sp.)*
snail, periwinkle *(Littorina sp.)*
    saltmarsh *(Malampus bidentatus)*
snake, black *(Coluber constrictor)*
spider *(Araneida)*
turtle, snapping *(Chelydra serpentina)*
    spotted *(Clemmys guttata)*
water bug, giant *(Lethocerus americanus)*

Common and Scientific Names of Plants

blackberry *(Rubus sp.)*
bulrush, salt-marsh *(Scirpus robustus)*
    softstem *(Scirpus validus)*
cattail, broadleaf *(Typha latifolia)*
    narrowleaf *(Typha angustifolia)*
celery, wild *(Vallisneria spiralis)*
cordgrass, big *(Spartina cynosuroides)*
    saltmarsh *(Spartina alterniflora)*
    saltmeadow *(Spartina patens)*
corn *(Zea mays)*
dogwood *(Cornus florida)*
eelgrass *(Zostera marina)*
grape *(Vitis spp.)*
grass, three-cornered *(Scirpus olneyi)*
greenbrier *(Smilax spp.)*
gum, black *(Nyssa sylvatica)*
honeysuckle, Japanese *(Lonicera japonica)*
ivy, poison *(Rhus radicans)*
mallow, rose *(Hibiscus moscheutos)*
    salt-marsh *(Kosteletzyka virginica)*
maple, red *(Acer rubrum)*
muskgrass *(Chara sp.)*
myrtle, wax *(Myrica cerifera)*
needlerush *(Juncus roemarianus)*

oak, pin *(Quercus palustris)*
    willow *(Quercus phellos)*
phragmites *(Phragmites communis)*
pickerelweed *(Pontederia cordata)*
pine, loblolly *(Pinus taeda)*
    shortleaf *(Pinus echinata)*
    Virginia *(Pinus virginiana)*
pondweed, sago *(Potamogeton pectinatus)*
rush, common or soft *(Juncus effusus)*
saltgrass *(Distichilis spicata)*
sassafras *(Sassafras albidum)*
sawgrass *(Cladium jamaicense)*
smartweed, dotted *(Polygonum punctatum)*
soybean *(Glycine soja)*
spikerush *(Eleocharis sp.)*
switchgrass *(Panicum virgatum)*
three-square, common *(Scirpus americanus)*
    Olney *(Scirpus olneyi)*
twigrush *(Cladium mariscoides)*
waterhemp, tidemarsh
    (Amaranthus cannabinus)
waterlily, white *(Nymphaea odorata)*
wheat *(Triticum aestivum)*
widgeongrass *(Ruppia maritima)*
wild rice *(Zizania aquatica)*

BIBLIOGRAPHY

(1) Jackson, R.W., 1941. "Breeding birds of the Cambridge area, Maryland." *Maryland Conservationist*, 18:22-26.

(2) Smith, F.R., 1938. *Muskrat investigations in Dorchester County, Maryland, 1930-1934.* U.S. Department of Agriculture Circular No. 474. Washington, D.C. 24 p.

(3) Stewart, R.E., 1962. *Waterfowl populations in the Upper Chesapeake region.* U.S. Department of the Interior, Fish and Wildlife Service—Wildlife No. 65. Washington, D.C. 208 p.

(4) Stewart, R.E., and C.S. Robbins, 1958. *Birds of Maryland and the District of Columbia.* North American Fauna 62. U.S. Department of the Interior. 401 p.

(5) Bonwill, A.H., 1941. Blackwater—a story of the marshlands in Dorchester County, Maryland. *Maryland Conservationist*, 18:14-15.

(6) Bellrose, F.C., 1976. *Ducks, geese & swans of North America.* Wildlife Management Institute and Illinois Natural History Survey. Stackpole Books, Harrisburg, Pennsylvania. 544 p.

(7) Addy, C.E., and J.D. Heyland, 1968. Canada goose management in Eastern Canada and the Atlantic Flyway, in *Canada goose management.* Edited by R.L. Hine and C. Schoenfeld. Dunbar Educational Research Services, Madison, Wisconsin. p. 10-23.

(8) Hanson, H.C., and C. Currie, 1952. The kill of wild geese by the natives of the Hudson-James Bay region. *Arctic*, 10:211-229.

(9) Palmer, R.S. (editor), 1976. *Handbook of North American birds.* Vol. 2. Yale University Press, New Haven, Connecticut. 521 p.

(10) Smith, F.R., 1936. The food and nesting habits of the bald eagle. *Auk*, 55:301-305.

(11) Bent, A.C., 1937. *Life histories of North American birds of prey.* (pt. 1). U.S. National Museum Bulletin 167. Smithsonian Institution, Washington, D.C. 409 p.

(12) Imler, R.H., and E.R. Kalmbach, 1955. *The bald eagle and its economic status.* Circular 30. Fish and Wildlife Service, U.S. Department of the Interior. 51 p.

(13) Lowery, G.H., Jr., 1974. *The mammals of Louisiana and its adjacent waters.* Louisiana Wild Life and Fisheries Commission. Louisiana State University Press. 565 p.

(14) O'Neil, T., 1949. *The muskrat in Louisiana coastal marshes.* Louisiana Department of Wild Life and Fisheries, New Orleans, Louisiana. 152 p.

Bibliography

(15) Harris, Van T., 1953. Ecological relationships of meadow voles and rice rats in tidal marshes. *Journal of Mammalogy*, 34:479-487.

(16) Harris, Van T., 1952. *Muskrats on tidal marshes of Dorchester County.* Publication no. 91. Chesapeake Biological Laboratory, Solomons Island, Maryland. 36 p.

(17) Taylor, John W., 1976. The woodcock. *Virginia Wildlife.* Commission of Game and Inland Fisheries, Richmond, Virginia. 37:27.

(18) Sheldon, W.G., 1967. *The book of the American woodcock.* University of Massachusetts Press, Amherst, Massachusetts. 227 p.

(19) Austin, O.L., Jr., 1932. Breeding of the blue-winged teal in Maryland. *Auk*, 49:191-198.

(20) Stewart, R.E., and J.W. Aldrich, 1956. Distinction of maritime and prairie populations of blue-winged teal. *Proceedings of the Biological Society of Washington*, 69:29-36.

(21) Stotts, V.E., and D.E. Davis, 1960. The black duck in the Chesapeake Bay of Maryland: Breeding behavior and biology. *Chesapeake Science*, 1:127-254.

(22) Stotts, V.E., 1957. Banding black ducks in Maryland. *Maryland Conservationist*, 34:16-20.

(23) Robbins, C.S. (compiler), 1974. Seventy-fourth Christmas bird count (Southern Dorchester County, Maryland). *American Birds*, 28:276-277.

(24) Reese, J.G., 1975. Diurnal vocalization by a wintering black rail. *Maryland Birdlife*, 31:13-14.

(25) Springer, P.F., and R.E. Stewart, 1948. Twelfth breeding-bird census; tidal marshes. *Audubon Field Notes*, 2:223-226.

(26) Meanley, B., and J.S. Webb, 1960. *Variation in population density and productivity of red-winged blackbirds in relation to habitat.* Progress report in files of U.S. Fish and Wildlife Service. 23 p.

(27) Lee, D.S., A. Norden, and B. Rothgaber, 1972. A preliminary analysis of the feeding habits of barn owls at Irish Grove Sanctuary. *Maryland Birdlife*, 28:27-28.

(28) Wilder, N., H. Cofer, and R. Beck, 1951. *The marsh raccoon as a competitor of the muskrat.* Final Report PR Project 9R, June. Delaware Board of Game and Fish Commissioners, Dover, Delaware. 5 p.

(29) Bent, A.C., 1938. *Life histories of North American birds of prey.* (pt. 2.) U.S. National Museum Bulletin 170. Smithsonion Institution, Washington, D.C., 409 p.

(30) Blogg, P.T., 1944. *There are no dull dark days.* H.G. Roebuck and Sons, Baltimore, Maryland. 92. p.

(31) Armistead, H., 1976. Middle Atlantic Coast region (F.R. Scott, editor). *American Birds*. National Audubon Society, New York, N.Y. 30:940.

(32) Cottam, C., and P. Knappen, 1939. Food of some uncommon North American birds. *Auk*, 56:138-169.

(33) Henny, C.J., 1972. *An analysis of the population dynamics of selected avian species.* U.S. Department of the Interior, Fish and Wildlife Service, Wildlife Research Report 1. Washington, D.C. 99 p.

(34) Hackman, C.D., and C.J. Henny, 1971. Hawk migration over White Marsh, Maryland. *Chesapeake Science*, 12:137-141.

(35) Stewart, R.E., and T.H. Manning, 1958. Distribution and ecology of whistling swans in the Chesapeake Bay region. *Auk*, 75:203-212.

(36) Sladen, W.J.L., W.W. Cochran, and R. Vose, 1974. Spring migration of the whistling swan. In *A Conference on the Biological Aspects of the Bird/Aircraft Collision Problem.* Clemson University, Clemson, South Carolina. p. 233-234.

(37) Burton, B., 1977. "Freezing weather hard on nutria." *The Evening Sun* (January 19). Baltimore, Maryland. p. D6.

(38) Julian, W.H., 1972. Swallow-tailed kite at Blackwater Refuge. *Maryland Birdlife*, 28:104.

(39) Robbins, C.S., 1973. The Season (October, November, December 1972). *Maryland Birdlife*, 29:26.

(40) Rhodes, Leon, 1970. White pelican seen at Blackwater Refuge. *Maryland Birdlife*, 26:3.

Index

Acorns, 22, 103
Aldrich, J.W., 57
American Birds, vii, 105
American Ornithologists' Union, 57
Amphibians, 9
Anne Arundel County, 19, 22
Arbib, Robert, vii
Armistead, Henry, 100
Arnold, Md., 19, 22
Atlantic blue-winged teal (*See* Blue-winged teal)
Atlantic Flyway, ix, x, 10, 17
Audubon Field Notes, 105
Auk, 19, 57
Austin, Oliver, 57

Baffin Island, 16, 18
Bald eagle, xi, 19-25, 30, 44, 46, 47, 120
    Christmas count, 105, 108
    density, 19
    flight, 22
    food, 23, 85
        analysis table, 24
    nest, ix, 2
        construction, 22
        photo, 20, 21
        size, 19, 22
    nesting season, 25
    perch, 9
Baltimore oriole, 58
Banded birds, 12, 76
    king rail, 70, 71
Bell, Elizabeth, vii
Bellrose, F.C., 113, 114
Bent, Arthur C., 22, 23, 93, 95, 97
Bestpitch, 7, 8
Big cordgrass (*See* Cordgrass)
Bird count (*See* Christmas bird count)
Birds of Maryland and the District of Columbia, 124, 130
Birds of prey, 85-88
Birds (*See* Breeding birds)
Bishop's Head, 1
Bittern
    American, 75
        migration, 98
    least, 3, 69, 75
Blackbird, red-winged, 3, 4, 7, 35, 61, 75, 76, 88, 122, 123
    female, photo, 62
    migration, 98, 99, 102, 103
    nesting sites, 59
    nest, photo, 63
    population density, 78, 105
Black duck, 66, 79
    drawing, 80
    eggs, 91
    food analysis, 83, 84
    habitat, 69, 81
    male population density, 78
    nesting habitat, 5
        photo, 65
    nesting season, 61
    photo, 64
Black rail (*See* Rail)
Blackwater Migratory Bird Refuge, 22

Blackwater National Wildlife Refuge, 1-4, 14, 15, 17 (*See also* individual entries)
    acreage, x
    bald eagles, 19-25
    bird count (*See* Christmas bird count)
    birds of prey, 85-88
    breeding birds, 39-47
        marsh, 59-78
    cordgrass, 5
    creation, ix
    deer, 89, 90
    Delmarva fox squirrel, 34-38
    development, x
    geese, 8, 13, 16-18
        migration, 12
    managers, x, xii (*See also* Managers)
    map, ii
    marsh ducks, 79-84
    migration, bird, 98-103
    muskrat research, 6, 26-31
        number trapped, 30
    nutria, 32, 33
    otter, 89, 90
    raccoons, 89, 91
    rare birds, 124-130
    swamp owl, 92-97
    swan, 113-117
    timberdoodle, 53-56
    wildlife drive, 9
    winter, 1977, 118-123
    wintering ground, 18
    woodpecker, 48-52
Blackwater River, xii, 1-3, 7, 12, 19, 33, 44, 57, 67, 68, 72, 73, 75, 77, 79, 101, 112
    location, ii
Blogg, P.T., 97
Bluebird, 39, 40, 44
    Christmas count, 108, 110
    migration, 98
Blue jay, 44, 97
Blue-winged teal, 4, 57-59, 75, 79
    drawing, 80
    male population density, 78
    migration, 98, 100
    nesting habitat, 5, 57, 81
    nest, photo, 59
Bobolink, 4
Bobwill, Allen, 1
Bond, Gorman, vii
Book of the American Woodcock, 54
Breeding birds, 39-47
    male population density, 78
    marsh, 59-78
Bufflehead, 79, 120
Bullock's oriole, 58
Bulrush, softstem, 3, 8
Burton, Bill, 122
Bystrak, Danny, vii

Cambridge, Md., 1, 119, 120
Canada goose, ix, 8, 14, 18, 90, 115, 117, 118, 130 (*See also* Goose)
    food, 4, 6
    migration, 11, 98-100
    speed, 15

Canada goose *(cont.)*
  on ice, photo, 119
  population, 8, 12, 105
Canvasback, 79, 121
  photo, 120
Cardinal, 44, 45
Carlson, Carl W., 126
Carp, 25
Carrion, 23
Catbirds, Christmas count, 108, 110
Cattail, 22, 33, 61
  broadleaf, 68, 69, 73
  narrowleaf, 3, 6, 8, 33, 59, 68, 89
Caulk, Elizabeth, vii
Central Flyway, 8
Chapman, Frank M., 104
Chesapeake Bay, ii, 1, 17, 19, 113-115, 118, 130
  Country, ix, 10, 12, 19, 57, 58, 68, 78, 82, 98, 100, 113, 116-118
Chester River, 12
Chickadees, Carolina, 39, 40, 44
Choptank River, 12, 79, 113, 115, 117, 119, 120
  location, ii
Christmas bird count, vii, xi, 44, 50, 55, 66, 67, 97, 121, 122, 124, 126
  southern Dorchester, 104-112, 133-136
    bluebirds, 108, 110
    catbirds, 108, 110
    Cooper's hawk, 111, 112
    eagles, 105, 108
    finches, 108
    owls, 110
    procedures, 104
    rails, 111
    robins, 108, 110
    shorebirds, 108
    thrashers, 108, 110
    warblers, 108
Chuck-will's-widow, 40, 45
  eggs, 44
  illustration, 43
Church Creek, 73, 115-117
Clams, 73, 91, 115, 117, 121
Clapper rail *(See* Rail)
Common gallinule *(See* Gallinule)
Common rush *(See* Rush)
Cooper's hawk, 111 *(See also* Hawk)
  photo, 110
Cordgrass
  big, 7, 8, 65
  saltmarsh, 4, 6, 7, 33, 59-61, 63, 67, 75, 90
  saltmeadow, 5-7, 59, 60, 75, 76, 81
Corn, 10, 12, 18, 22, 35, 37, 81, 90, 91, 97, 116, 119, 121
Cowbird, brown-headed, 44
  migration, 102
Crab, 90, 91, 112
  blue, 23
  mud, 73
  red-jointed fiddler, 73
  soft, 83
Crane, Stanley, 127
Crayfish, 68, 73, 90, 95, 97
Crow, 46, 66, 91, 95, 96 *(See also* Fish crow)
Crustaceans, 9, 79, 83, 90

Dabblers *(See* Ducks)
Davis, David E., 61, 91
DeCoursey Bridge, 4, 6, 7, 67
Deer, 89, 90
  drawing, 90

Delaware Conservationist, vii
Delaware Game and Fish Commission, 31
Delmarva fox squirrel, ix, 34-38, 97 *(See also* Squirrels)
  food, 35, 37
  habitat, 34, 36
  nest, 38
  photo, 34
  population, 34
  size, 35
Denmead, Talbot, xi, 57
Dogwood, 90, 102
Dorchester County, Md., vii, ix, 1, 4, 7, 19, 33, 34, 40, 46, 57-59, 75-77, 79, 81, 83, 84, 87, 90, 97, 103, 115, 117, 120, 121, 123, 130
  Christmas bird count, 104-112, 133-136
    nuthatch, chart, 107
    snow goose, chart, 106
    commercial trappers, 30
Dove, mourning, 44
  nesting season, 47
  nest, photo, 47
Dozier, Herbert L., xii, 32
Ducks, 23, 119 *(See also* individual ducks, i.e., Mallard, etc.)
  fulvous tree, 124, 128
  marsh, 79-84
    dabblers, 79, 81, 118
    diving, 79, 121
    food, 79
  whistling, 127
  wood, 45
DuMont, Paul G., 126
DuMont, Philip, 126
Dunkeson, Larry, 125
Dunlins, 9
  migration, 98

Eagle *(See* Bald eagle; Golden Eagle)
Eastern Neck National Wildlife Refuge, 34
Eelgrass, 63, 83
Egrets, 9
  cattle, 98, 101, 130
  great (American), 98, 101
  migration, 100
  photo, 33
  snowy, 98, 101
Egypt Road, 19
Elliott Island, 33, 66, 109, 117, 121, 122
  bird count, 104

Falcon, peregrine, 127
  photo, 126
Fall migration *(See* Migration)
Fescue, 18
Finches, northern, 108
Fish crow, 40, 44
Fishing Bay, ii, 1, 2, 7, 33, 66, 67, 79, 112
  Wildlife Management Area, 122
Flamingo, 127
Flicker, 44, 95, 97
Florio, Tony, vii, 31
Flycatchers, crested, 39, 40, 44, 45
  migration, 100
Food, stomach analysis, 83
  chart, 84
Foxes, 30
Fresh Bay marsh, 3
Fuertes, L.A., 25, 87, 109, 110
Fulvous tree duck, 124, 127
  photo, 128

Index

Gadwall, 79
  drawing, 80
  habitat, 81
Gallinule, common, 3
  photo, 67
Gannet, 112
Geise, Bill, 36
George, Sam, 65
Gnatcatcher, blue-gray, 44
  migration, 98
Golden eagle, 105, 108
Goldeneye, 79
Golden Hill, 48
Goldman, Luther C., vii, 13, 17, 67, 101, 104, 121
Goose blind, 15
  tree-house, 14, 15
Goose (*See also* Canada goose; Snow goose)
  blue, 16
  Canada, ix, 10, 13, 15
    migration, 11
    population, 12, 105
    weight, 10
  Egyptian, 127
  food, 4, 6
  population, 8, 10
  snow, 8, 16-18, 105
Grackle
  boat-tailed, 111, 112
    photo, 111, 112
  bronzed, 58
    migration, 103
  common, 35, 87, 105
    migration, 102, 103
    photo, 111
  purple, 58
    migration, 103
Green-winged teal, 79
  drawing, 80
  habitat, 81
  migration, 98, 100
Grimes, Sam A., vii, 43
Gulls
  herring, 130
  laughing, 98
  ring-billed, 98, 117
Gum, black, 90, 102
Gum Swamp, 1, 19, 22, 23, 68, 72, 73, 97
  location, ii
Gum trees, 19
Gyrfalcon, 124-127

Hackman, C.D., 111
Hahn, Robert, 126
Hamlet, John, 45
Haramis, Mike, vii, 42, 117, 120
Hardwood swamp, 92, 93, 96, 100
Harrier (*See* Hawks, marsh)
Harrison, Harry N., xi
Harris, Van T., xii, 6, 30, 86, 91
Hawks, 30, 85, 87
  Cooper's, Christmas count, 111
    photo, 110
  marsh, drawing, 85
    pellets, 86
  red-shouldered, 85, 93, 95
    nest and eggs, photo, 96
  red-tailed, 23, 44, 46, 85, 97
Hemp, tidemarsh water, 8, 33
Henny, C.J., 111
Herons, 9
  blue, 101, 121, 122
  Louisiana, 101
  migration, 100
Herrick, Prof., 23
Hibiscus, 6, 7 (*See also* Rose mallow)
Hightide-bush, 79
Hines, Bob, vii, 80, 85, 89-91
Holly, American, 40
Honga River, 68, 69, 79
Hooper Island, ii, 1, 73, 110, 112
Hoover, Charlotte, 127
Howe, Marshall, vii, 74
Hudson Bay, 11, 12, 17
Hummingbird, 88, 100
Hunting season, 15
Hurlock, P., 48

Ibises, 9
  glossy, 98, 130
  photo, 129
Imler, R.H., 23
Insley, Curtis, 28

Jackson, Ralph, x, 45, 46, 47, 61, 67, 68, 97
Jacobs, J. Warren, 22
James Bay, 11, 12, 17
Japanese honeysuckle, 90
Jewelweed, 100
Julian, William H., vii, x, 21, 34, 46, 48, 51, 86, 122, 125-127, 129, 130

Kalmbach, E.R., 23
Kentuck Swamp, 1
Killdeer, 98
Kingbirds, 39
  migration, 100
Kingfisher, 122
King rail (*See* Rail)
Kirkwood, F.C., 77
Kite, swallow-tailed, 124
  photo, 125

Lapland longspur, 112
Larvae
  mosquito, 9
  moth, 8
Least bittern (*See* Bittern)
Lee, D.S., 88
Life Histories of North American Birds of Prey, 93
Little Blackwater River, xii, 1, 23, 33, 57, 68, 79
  location, ii
Little Choptank River, location, ii
Loblolly pine forests, 1, 2, 9, 19, 20, 36, 38, 48, 50, 52, 92
  breeding birds, 39-47
    nesting season, 46
Lowery, G.H., 32, 33, 89

Mallard, 79
  drawing, 80
  habitat, 81
  migration, 100
Mallow
  rose, 6, 7
  saltmarsh, 6, 7
Managers, Blackwater Refuge (*See also* individual names)
  Julian, William H., vii, x
  Van Huizen, Peter J., x, xii
  Wallace, Cornelius, x
Manning, T.H., 115
Maple, 90

Marsh, 22, 78, 92 (*See also* Cordgrass; Needlerush; Olney; Switchgrass)
  burning, 5, 6
  fresh Bay, 3
  Olney three-square brackish, 2, 3, 4, 6-8, 18, 59, 122
Marsh ducks (*See* Ducks)
Martin, A.C., 82
Martins, purple, 98
Maryland Birdlife, 125
Maryland Conservationist, xi
Maryland Game and Inland Fish Commission, 57, 91
McIlhenny, E.A., 32
Meanley, Anna Gilkeson, vii, 71
Meekins Creek, ii, 1, 79
Mergansers, 79
  common, 79
  hooded, 79
  red-breasted, 79
Mice (*See* Voles)
Migration, 98-103 (*See also* Migration listed under various bird entries)
Migration corridor, 11
  Mid-Atlantic, 12
  swan, 114
Millet, 33
Mills, Orrille, 77
Mink, 30
Minnows, 9, 81
Mollusks, 9, 83, 115, 116
Molt, summer, 18
Moneystump Swamp, 1, 97
"Monks," 87
Mosquito larvae, 9, 81
Muskgrass, 79, 117
  photo, 83
Muskrat, x, xii, 23, 26-31, 86, 88, 90, 122, 123
  "double house," 30
  "eatouts," 8, 29, 30
  food, 4, 27
  house, 2, 85, 89, 127
    photo, 28, 29
  litter, 30
  number trapped, 30
  overpopulation, 30
  photo, 26
  plunge hole, 27, 28
  predators, 30, 91
  research, 6
  size, 26
  trap, 22
Myrtle, wax, 40
  berries, photo, 102

Names (*See* Scientific names)
National Audubon Society, vii, 104, 105
Needlerush plant, 59, 60, 68, 69, 112, 118
Nelson, Arnold, 66
Nesting season, 75 (*See also* Nesting season listed under various birds)
Nests, false, 77
  photo, 76
Nicholson, W.R., 75
Norden, Arnold, 88
Nuthatches
  brown-headed, 39-41, 44, 105, 111
    nest, 43
    winter population, chart, 107
Nutria, 6, 32, 33, 122
  habitat, 33
  photo, 32
  size, 32

Oak trees, 19, 90, 103
Olney three-square brackish marsh, 2-4, 7, 8, 33, 59, 61, 76, 79, 81 (*See also* Marsh)
  burning, 5, 59
  muskrat habitat, 6, 27, 29
O'Neil, T., 30
Oriole
  Baltimore, 58
  Bullock's, 58
  orchard, 100
Osprey, 19, 23, 25
  migration, 98
  nest, 86
Otter, 89, 90
  drawing, 89
Ovenbird, 44, 45
  migration, 100
Owl, 105
  barn, 85
  barred (swamp), 85, 92-97
    nest and eggs, photo, 94
    photo, 92-96
  Christmas count, 110
  food, 88
  great horned, 22, 40, 44, 47, 85, 93
    photo, 45, 46
  long-eared, 87
  screech, 16, 17, 85
    food, 87
    photo, 87
  short-eared, 77
    drawing, 85
  young, photo, 86

Palmer, R.S., 114
Patuxent Wildlife Research Center, 83
Peenting, 54
Pelican, white, 124, 127
Periwinkle snails, 22, 69
Perry, Matthew C., vii, 50, 56, 64, 73, 83, 121, 124
Pewee, wood, 44
Phoebe, migration, 98
Phragmites, ix, 8
Pickerelweed, 8
Pigeons, 102, 103
Pine swamps, 92
Pine tree (*See* Loblolly, Virginia, Shortleaf)
Pintail, 79, 84
  drawing, 80
  migration, 100
Plover, 100
Poison ivy, 102, 121
Ponds, 9
Pondweed, 115-117
Puddle ducks (*See* Ducks)
Pungo National Wildlife Refuge, N.C., 35

Rabbits, 46
Raccoons, 30, 89, 91
  drawing, 91
Rail, 27, 90, 105
  black, 5, 7, 67
    adult, photo, 66
    nest, 66
  brownish king, 67
  Carolina, 100
  Christmas count, 111
  clapper, 7, 67
    drawing, 68
    habitat, 69
  grayish clapper, 67
  king, 3, 6, 7, 46, 67, 70, 71, 91
    habitat, 6, 73

Rail *(cont.)*
    nesting season, 68
    nest, photo, 69, 72
    sora, 4, 67
        migration, 100
    Virginia, 3, 67, 88
        nesting site, 59
Rare birds, 124-130
Rats
    brown, 88
    house, 88
    rice, 27, 30, 77, 86, 88
Red-cockaded woodpecker (*See* Woodpecker)
Redhead, 79
Redheart, 48
Red-winged blackbird (*See* Blackbird)
Reese, Jan, 66, 111
Regurgitated pellets, 85, 87 (*See also* Food)
Rice, 4, 127
Robbins, Chandler S., vii, xi, xii, 75, 77, 78
Robin
    Christmas count, 108
    migration, 98, 103
Rose mallow, 6
    blooming period, 7
Rothgaber, Barbara, 88
Rowlett, 126
Ruddy duck, 79
Rush, common, 68, 73

Saltmarsh bulrush, 79, 81
Saltmarsh cordgrass (*See* Cordgrass)
Saltmarsh mallow, 6
    blooming period, 7
Saltmarsh meadow (*See* Cordgrass)
Saltmeadow cordgrass (*See* Cordgrass)
Sandpiper, 100
Sapsucker, 121
Sassafras, 90
Scaup, 79
Scheffer, V.B., 26
Schmid, Frederick C., 92, 103
Schmidt, Rex Gary, 10
Scientific names
    animals, 139
    birds, 137, 138
    mammals, 139
    plants, 139
Screech owl (*See* Owl)
Seaside sparrow (*See* Sparrow)
Seaweed, 83
Sedge, 50, 62, 90
    three-cornered, 4, 10
Sewards, 68
Sharp-tailed sparrow (*See* Sparrow)
Sheldon, William G., 54
Shoal-water ducks (*See* Ducks)
Shorebirds, 9, 75
    Christmas count, 108
    migration, 100
Shorter's Landing, 57
Shorter's Wharf, 66, 76, 101
Shortleaf pine, 50
Shoveler, 79
    drawing, 80
    habitat, 81
    migration, 98, 100
Shrews, 88
Sladen, William, 117
Smartweed, dotted, 8, 81
Smilax, 90
Smith, Frank R., xi, xii, 19, 22, 23, 28, 30, 48, 86, 88

Snails, 79, 81, 103
Snake, black, 55
Snipe, 9
    migration, 98
Snow goose, 8, 13, 16-18, 115 (*See also* Goose)
    lesser, 8, 13
    migration, 18, 100
    population, 17
    wintering ground, 17
        population, 106
Snyder, Noel, 125
Sora (*See* Rail)
Southern Dorchester County Christmas Bird Count, 133-136 (*See also* Christmas bird count)
Soybeans, 12, 18, 37, 90, 115, 116, 119, 121
Sparrow
    Bachman's, 112
    seaside, 5, 75, 76
        male population density, 78
        migration, 98
        nest and eggs, photo, 60
        nesting habitat, 61
    sharp-tailed, 5, 75, 76
        male population density, 78
Spikerush, 8
Springer, P.F., 78
Spring migration (*See* Migration)
Squirrels, 46, 88, 95
    Delmarva fox, ix, 34-38 (*See also* Delmarva fox squirrel)
    Eastern fox, 35
    flying, 41
    gray, 34-38
Stanley crane, 127
Starling, 97
State list, 124, 126
Steenis, J.H., 75
Stewart, G. Wallace, 127
Stewart, Robert E., vii, xi, xii, 48, 57, 66, 75, 77-79, 83, 84, 115, 124
Stilt, black-necked, 124
Stotts, Vern, 61, 66, 91
Swallows, 100, 111
    tree, 39-41
        migration, 98, 101, 102
        nest, 42
        photo, 41, 42
Swamp rose, 73
Swan, whistling, 12, 18, 118, 120
    feeding, photo, 116
    migration, 98, 113, 115
        corridor, 114
    wintering ground, 113-117
        photo, 113, 119
        population, 113
Switchgrass, 3, 50, 68, 73

Tanager, summer, 44
Taylor, John W., vii, xi, 53, 104, 113, 117, 123
Teal (*See* Blue-winged; Green-winged)
Tern, gull-billed, 124
Thrashers, 108, 110
Thrush, 105
    migration, 100
    Swainson's, 112
    wood, 44
Timberdoodle, 53-56, 95, 97
    breeding grounds, 54
    chick, 56
    clutch, 55
    migration, 98
    nest, photo, 55, 56

Timberdoodle *(cont.)*
  peenting, 54
  wintering grounds, 55
Titmouse, tufted, 39, 44
Towhee, 45, 46
  rufous-sided, 44
Transquaking River, xii, 1, 3, 4, 6, 7, 33, 67, 79, 99
  location, ii
Tree duck (*See* Fulvous tree duck)
Tregoe, W.G., 57
Twigrush, 8, 79, 81
Tyrell, W.B., 23

Uhler, Francis, vii, x, xi, 8, 66, 82, 83
Ungava Peninsula, 11, 12, 99
U.S. Biological Survey, xii, 57
U.S. Fish and Wildlife Service, vii, x, xi, xii, 6, 10, 13, 17, 21, 25, 26, 32, 34, 42, 48, 53, 56, 64, 67, 73, 74, 80, 83, 85, 87, 89-92, 99, 101, 103, 109, 110, 117, 120, 121, 126

Van Huizen, Peter J., vii, x, xii, 19, 22, 53, 55, 68, 75, 124
Vireo, white-eyed, 44, 45
Virginia pine, 19, 22, 50, 124
Virginia rail (*See* Rail)
Virginia Wildlife, 53
Voles, meadow, 46, 85-88, 122
Vultures, 23

Wallace, Cornelius, x (*See also* Managers)
Walnuts, 37
Warbler, 105
  Christmas count, 108
  pine, 40, 44
    migration, 98
  prairie, migration, 100
  yellow, 39, 46, 109, 121
  yellow-throated, 44, 46
Warren, John, 77
Waterfowl Populations in the Upper Chesapeake Region, 84
Waterhemp, 8, 33
Waterlilies, 33, 90
  white, 3
Waterthrushes, migration, 98, 100
Wax myrtle, 73, 101, 109, 121
  berries, 102
Webb, J.S., 78
Webster, Clark, 66
Wheat, winter, 12, 116
  field, 115

Whistling swan (*See* Swan)
Widgeongrass, 79, 81, 115-117
  drawing, 82
Wigeon, 79, 83
  drawing, 80
  habitat, 81
  migration, 100
Wild celery, 115
Wild rice, 4, 127
Wilds, Claudia, 66
Willet, 68
  male population density, 78
  migration, 98
  nest and eggs, 74, 75
  nesting habitat, 5
  wing pattern, photo, 74
Willey, Guy, vii, x, 19, 36, 37, 50, 51, 122
Winter, 1977, 118-123
Wintering grounds, 113-117 (*See also* Migration)
Woodcock (*See* Timberdoodle)
Wood ducks, 45 (*See also* Ducks)
Wood mice, 88
Woodpeckers, 40
  downy, 50
  flicker, 50
  hairy, 44
  pileated, 44, 45, 50, 52
  red-bellied, 44, 50
  red-cockaded, x, xi, 40, 48-52, 53, 105, 112, 124, 130
    habitat, 48
    history, 48
    markings, 48
    nest, 49
    nesting requirements, 50
  red-headed, 44
Wren
  Carolina, 44
  house, 39, 40, 44
    migration, 100
  long-billed marsh, 3, 76, 78
    female, photo, 77
    nesting habitat, 7
    nest, photo, 61
  marsh, breeding male, 78
  short-billed marsh, 75, 78, 111
    false nest, photo, 76
Wye River, 12

Yellowlegs, 9
  migration, 98
Yellowthroat, 44, 45